Achieving Excellence in Our Schools

. . . by Taking Lessons from America's Best-Run Companies

Achieving Excellence in Our Schools

... by Taking Lessons from America's Best-Run Companies

James Lewis, Jr.

J. L. Wilkerson Publishing Company
Westbury, New York

Library of Congress Cataloging-in-Publication Data

Lewis, James, Jr., 1930–
Achieving Excellence in Our Schools—by Taking Lessons
    from America's Best-Run Companies

    Bibliography: p.
    Includes Index.
    1. Education—United States—Aims and objectives.
2. Education—United States—Philosophy. 3. School
management and organization—United States. I. Title.
LA217.L48 1986   370'.973   85-51152
ISBN 0-915253-03-8

• ACKNOWLEDGMENT •

I am indebted to numerous people who helped make this book a reality. I especially owe a great deal of gratitude to the corporate, school, and community people who shared information and materials with me. These people, many of whom must remain anonymous, gave generously of their time and insights (I promised them anonymity in return for their candor).

I owe much to my wife, Valdmir, and my children, Michael, Patricia, and Terence, for their unfailing love, patience and encouragement even when I spent endless weeknights and weekends having to absent myself from their presence to collect my thoughts and write this book.

Finally, I would like to thank Thomas and Daisy Eddy for their preparation of this manuscript. My penmanship is atrocious—it takes people with patience and fortitude to decipher each word and sentence. I am deeply indebted to my editor, Stacy Hinck, for her creative insights and superior skills. I know the book reads better as a result of her unique abilities.

James Lewis, Jr.
New York

To my daughter
Patricia Mary Lewis
who is striving so diligently
to make a contribution to humanity

• CONTENTS •

• HALLMARKS OF EXCELLENCE •

The following is a partial list of characteristics that distinguish an excellent school district. It is provided to give you food for thought and action so that you can forge your own path to excellence.

Excellence is

- a school district in which all school people are helping kids to become something more than they ever hoped to be.

- a school district that provides incentives for developing innovations and programs that improve students' learning and growth.

- a school district that not only welcomes new ideas but also rewards the school people who offer them.

- a school district that integrates all parts of the school organization—strategy, human resources, capital assets, reward systems, structure, marketing, and promotion—into a cohesive and manageable whole.

- a school district with a superintendent who creates an organizational culture and structure in which the talents of all school people may flourish.

- a school district with a board that avoids getting involved in day-to-day administrative decisions, choosing instead to monitor the major decisions of the central administrative team to ensure that they are consistent with the philosophy and vision of the school district.

- a school district with a superintendent who preaches the philosophy of the school district, who pays attention to the school district's strengths and avoids its weaknesses, and who talks about the future and vision of the school district to all school and community people.

- a school district that has become a learning organization.

- a school district that has the courage to change things even when all is going well, the courage to require its administrators to share power and authority with school people, the courage to stick with its values during difficult times, the courage to rely less on short-term results and more on long-term gains, and the courage to involve all school people at all levels of the organization to improve performance and solve problems.

- a school district with a supertindent who treats all school people with as much respect as he or she does members of the board of education.

- a school district that backs its commitment to training and development with dollars.

- a school district that gives school people freedom to take risks, question long-standing principles and practices, and try new things.

• INTRODUCTION •

It Takes Guts to Achieve Excellence

The adventuring of excellence is not for the faint of heart.
— TOM PETERS AND NANCY AUSTIN

The best-run companies in America, such as IBM, Hewlett-Packard, Delta Air Lines, General Electric, and Dana, embody excellence. How were they able to accomplish this feat? Did they provide quality products and services to their customers? Did they enjoy a strong culture? Did they out-perform their competitors? Did they consistently increase growth and earnings? Did they treat their people well? They did all of these and much more. They encouraged experimentation and innovation in a constant quest to meet the needs and expectations of their customers; they were never satisfied with their current level of performance; they provided their people with freedom and flexibility to perform their jobs; and they recognized, praised and rewarded not only managers, but all of their people who achieved above-plan performance.

Excellence in education can be judged by both objective and subjective criteria. Objective criteria of excellence would most likely include academic achievement scores; student and teacher attendance rate; scores on the SATs; number of students admitted to colleges and universities; number of students receiving scholarship awards; average cost to educate a student; number of library books per student; and dropout rate. Subjective criteria of excellence could include quality of school management; quality of instructional resources, teaching, and services; financial soundness; ability to attract, develop, and keep talented people; use of the school district resources; community responsibility; appropriateness of procedures for monitoring student learning and growth; parental involvement; and state of school district culture.

Although both objective and subjective criteria can help to identify excellent school districts, I believe that excellence is an elusive quality and that it therefore varies with the nature and stage of development of the school district. Thus, instead of adopting objective and/or subjective criteria, I recommend that each school district adopt specific performance standards by which to evaluate itself. As a result, tailormade performance standards for excellence may involve measurements of parental satisfaction with the performance of the school district; rank in terms of the students'academic achievement scores relative to those of students in contiguous school districts; assessment of innovations that enhance learning and growth of kids; evaluation of training designed to develop school administrators into leaders, etc. The important feature of my concept of excellence is that the standards selected, whatever their nature, must be stated in writing, mutually agreed to by a team of school and community people, and disseminated throughout the school and community. They must be used to demonstrate that the school district has become more each day than it was yesterday and ever hoped to become.

This book is about a theory formulated several years ago. It is not a new theory; it probably has been around for years. Although I recently read that Peter Drucker has also formalized this theory, I call my version of it the "success-emulation" theory. The basis of this theory is the view that either a person or an organization can attain success or excellence by studying the products, principles, and practices of successful organizations and then adopting those that are appropriate to the new situation with or without modifications.

The Japanese are noted for being excellent success emulators. They are known for studying a product or practice in minute detail to determine its strengths and weaknesses, then improving on the strengths and turning the weaknesses into strengths. U.S. companies are also known to be excellent in emulating success. If you question what I am saying, just visit any computer store and see how many personal computers resemble or are compatible with the IBM PC. If you think that Kodak created its own instant camera without studying Polaroid's camera, you had better think again.

The success-emulation theory provides an ideal procedure for pursuing a course for achieving excellence in our schools for two reasons:

- It saves time, money, and energy because it does not involve months or years of experimentation, and because it ensures that the changes instituted have the potential to work successfully.

- It gives an organization an advantage over the originator of the product, practice, or principle being emulated, because the emulator can direct limited funds and more attention to eliminating weaknesses or accommodating specific needs through modification of the original product, practice, or principle. The emulation of successful products, principles, or practices often leads to the development of new and creative ones.

Recently a runaway best-seller entitled *In Search of Excellence* revealed the results of a study of the best-run companies in America. Thomas J. Peters and Robert H. Waterman, the co-authors of this classic, maintain that our best-run companies tend to be process- and result-oriented and to treat people as their greatest resource. These companies offer job security, promotion based on excellent performance, and internal training and development. They provide a multitude of opportunities for employees to participate meaningfully in the decision-making process. They regard their people as associates, team members, or partners, rather than merely employees. They promote a common value system that perpetuates excellence and contributes to their people's well-being. These companies understand the wisdom of relying heavily on individual and team innovation and creative energy. In these companies, the individual employee is used to the fullest extent of his or her creativity through participation methods such as teamwork, suggestion boxes, consensus decision-making groups, quality circles, and a host of other activities.

The organizations of the best-run companies are organic and entrepreneurial instead of mechanistic and bureaucratic. They are less planned, less rigid, but value driven to common purposes. One of the essential differences between the best-run companies and the "others" is that the best-run companies start with their people, trusting them as human beings and trusting their capability and their potential. In essence, they are people sensitive.

By taking lessons from our best-run companies, we can carry out our quest for excellence in our school districts expeditiously, humanely, and with less money. However, some school board members and superintendents may not have either the desire or the stamina to do what it will take to move along the path to excellence.

It takes guts to achieve excellence in our schools. Outmoded ways have become too much of a habit for us to give them up without much pain. Too many state education officials, school board members, superintendents, school administrators, union officials, teachers, and other school people (including parents) have been comfortable for far too long with the manner in which our school districts are being managed. At times, the path to excellence will be uphill, bumpy, treacherous, and scary. There will be many times when you will ask yourself, "Is excellence worth all this labor, grief, and agony?"

I say to you, "Yes! Our kids are our greatest asset, and we must do all that is humanly possible to bring them the best education possible. But your job will not be easy!"

It will take guts for the board of education to question the motives of misdirected board members and condemn them when they perform an act injurious to the school district. The board will need to be courageous to take public abuse from dissident community members who are not interested in moving in the direction of excellence. The board will need determination to demand that incompetent school administrators decide either to get in the path of excellence or to get out of the school district. The board will need endurance to put in the long and arduous hours and the energy that will be necessary to acquire and apply new knowledge and skills.

It will take guts for the superintendent to examine everything that he or she is presently doing, to compare it with the principles and practices that work well in business and industry, and then to emulate the latter where appropriate. The superintendent will need to have the foresight to establish a succession program so that the board will have an ample supply of well-trained and well-developed general administrators from which to select a new superintendent.

The superintendent will need to be stout of heart to rotate an ineffectual principal to a "harmless" position when the opposition is strong, adamant, and abusive. The superintendent will need to make considerable effort to become people oriented rather than desk oriented, to unseat himself or herself from the office and wander around the organization as the CEOs of the best-run companies do. The superintendent will need to become a strategic thinker, to become proactive, and to assume risk rather than simply react to crises and emergencies.

It will take guts for a principal to organize his or her school people into teams and give them autonomy; it will take skill to plan, control, and manage the instructional process. A principal who was reluctant to share power will need self-confidence to begin sharing power with teachers and other school people. The principal will need to be a protector, providing a support system for school champions, because many people will not be aware of their value to the school system and may therefore feel threatened by them. The principal will need tenacity to meet with every school person at least once daily, talking, listening, and facilitating, because in the past principals have always had excuses for not meeting with school people on a consistent basis. The principal will need humility to view himself or herself as a support person for teachers, because previously he or she has in the role of overseer.

It will take guts for teachers too to trust their principal, because some principals in the past have not been worthy of trust. Teachers will need time to become heavily involved in acquiring new knowledge and skills, because many of the principles and practices of the best-run companies are new to education and teachers have limited experience with them. Teachers will need to develop the skills necessary to honestly evaluate their peers as team members, because previously they seldom had opportunity or encouragement to do so.

Teachers will need to be generous to commit themselves to going beyond the collective bargaining agreement in situations that warrant it, because school administrators' past behavior may not have encouraged them to "go beyond the call of duty."

It will take guts for parents to approve additional funds to develop excellence, because in many instances taxes have been increased without a corresponding increase in education. Parents will need to be forthright and critical of community members who use the school district as a platform for their own political gains. Parents will need to work to accept the notion that the school system includes the whole community, because parents sometimes have not been too responsive to the community-minded school administrators, as you will learn in this book. Parents will need understanding to realize that although they have had schooling, they may not have all of the answers to the new requirements for excellence in education and must therefore put their trust in their school people, the same kind of trust that stockholders place in the owners of the best-run companies in America.

If the board of education and the superintendent do decide to take the journey to educational excellence, they will need to reshape the attitudes of school and community people by showing them that the idea of achieving excellence requires more than lip service. School people will not believe that the administration is desirous of turning the school district around. They will begin to ask certain questions, such as: Will they provide us with tools that will be needed? Will they give us additional compensation? How will our jobs be affected? Is this another one shot deal? Not only will the superintendent experience some difficulties convincing school people, but there will be many community skeptics. The principals are likely to be the most critical and skeptical. To prove its commitment, the school district will have to do something extraordinary to convince them. One way to convince principals might be to establish a budget strictly for activities related to achieving excellence in the school district, from which funds would be expended based on an individual principal's efforts and commitment to excellence.

The best-run companies referred to in this book are for the most part the sixty-two companies cited in the book *In Search of Excellence* by Thomas J. Peters and Robert H. Waterman, Jr., the one hundred companies reported on in the book, *The Hundred Best Companies to Work for in America* by Robert Levering, Milton Moskowitz, and Michael Katz, and eight corporatives mentioned in *Vanguard Management* by James O'Toole. I have also used the book, *A Passion for Excellence*, by Tom Peters and Nancy Austin as an essential reference for substantiating the claims in many of the lessons covered in this book. A few other companies not listed in these books are included to illustrate a point or discuss successful practices.

The principles and practices of the best-run companies that were selected were those that could easily be adopted in public and private education. Obviously, it will take more time to implement some than it will others. No principle or practice should be adopted by a school district until it has been thoroughly studied. Planning for implementation must involve all of the people who will be affected by the change. In some instances, additional funds may be needed to implement a particular practice. Board members should not be penny wise and pound foolish. These practices will more than pay for themselves with their results.

Some new practices will enable school administrators to solve prevailing problems. Take, for example, the practice of restructuring the school district into teams and providing teachers with autonomy and the opportunity to engage in intrapreneurship. This practice alone can help solve the problem of poor management, ineffective performance evaluation, poor teaching, teacher absenteeism, and a host of other related problems. One of the benefits associated with adopting certain practices of the best-run companies is that they tend to be multi-dimensional in solving organization problems. If these principles and practices are implemented in a school district, school administrators will find their effectiveness increased, their behavior with school people improved, their self-esteem enhanced, and their managerial tasks simplified.

Some readers may ask, "Do the principles and practices of the best-run companies conflict with the research on school effectiveness?" My response to this question is an emphatic no. The principles and practices in this book capitalize on the essence of the research. For example, research indicates that effective schools have a clearly articulated mission. One of the lessons of this book explains how to produce not only a mission statement, but a complete statement of philosophy in which the mission is included, and then goes even further to discuss how to use the philosophy to inculcate a strong culture. To achieve excellence, one focuses not on the mission, but on the culture.

Recently, a number of reports have been circulated offering advice on achieving excellence in our schools. I applaud these reports for their insights. They recommend providing additional courses, adding years to some of the present course offerings, and a host of other changes. This book, however, will deal only with the people side of schooling, because I believe that when you give school people more freedom to perform, they will act more responsibly; they will be creative in solving school-related problems without being asked; they will provide an education agenda that is far superior to that which school administrators presently impose on them. What school administrators must do is to get out of the way of the people who will be solving the problems. They must begin to realize that their role should be to act as a coach, offering sound advice, motivating improved efforts, and providing proper support while the school district travels the path to achieve excellence.

I believe that most of the attributes of the excellent companies can be applied and adopted by U.S. public schools to achieve a high degree of excellence which has been far too long overdue. In this book, I will discuss twelve lessons that board members, school administrators, teachers, other school people, and parents can learn from the best-run companies. I am also in the process of writing a sequel to this book to cite more lessons we can learn from our best-run companies. Because many school people may be fixed or set in their ways, they will disagree with some of my assessments and recommendations. I have learned through many years of presenting seminars and speeches around the nation that many educators do not look kindly at someone who criticizes what presently is going on in our schools. My intent is not to be unkind or too critical, but to suggest how school people can learn from the lessons of America's best-run companies.

Periodically, I have cited certain incidents that have occurred in our schools to illustrate or clarify a point. I have avoided naming any person whose behavior was an impediment to excellence or any school district in which not so excellent practices occurred. I have included names of people and school districts that promote excellence in education in order to give credit where due.

Please note that I have included a glossary at the end of this book for those readers who may not be familiar with certain terms which I have used.

Strategies for Achieving Excellence

The first task in achieving excellence in a school district is for the superintendent to zero in on his or her vision of excellence. This will require the acquisition of new knowledge, training, and experiences. The initial step is to become acquainted with the principles and practices that the best-run companies have adopted, by reading this book in its entirety and the four other books mentioned in this introduction. Arrangements should be made for these books to be located in each school library for dissemination to school people; school administrators should be asked to read all five books for future reference.

To supplement this reading, the superintendent could charge a team of central administrators and supervisors with the responsibility for contacting the Department of Education in Washington, D.C., state departments of education, and noted personages in education to collect information on school districts that have successfully implemented innovative principles and practices. The superintendent should then study the materials and arrange to visit these schools with a cadre of school people. In addition, arrangements might be made for two central administrators and two principals to visit some of the best-run companies to learn how these organizations are managed.

By the time all of the recommended materials have been read and visitations have taken place, the superintendent should have a clear vision of how to achieve excellence in that particular school district. That vision of excellence should be the springboard for the following activities:

- Conduct a "Day of Excellence" meeting with the members of the school board to present a report on the principles and practices observed in both innovative school districts and the best-run companies. The objective of this meeting is for the superintendent to give the board a taste of what it can expect when it receives the district's long-range plan for achieving excellence.

- Conduct a series of six to nine biweekly meetings with school administrators at which the contents of the reading materials previously assigned are discussed and the substance of the reading is related to the principles and practices that were observed during the visitations. These sessions should generate a great amount of discussion and enthusiasm for the school district's quest for excellence.

- Organize a task force to prepare the long-range plan for excellence, considering the vision of the superintendent, the substance of the discussions with the school administrators, and the needs and constraints of the school district.

- Review the long-range plans for excellence, make revisions as necessary, and prepare a three- to five-page financial memorandum. Submit both of these plans to the school board as semifinal recommendations, to be finalized when input has been obtained from more school and community people.

- Convene a special meeting with the community to illuminate all aspects of the long-range plan for achieving excellence. Written materials and audiovisual aids should be highly professional, representing the beginning of excellence. A secretary should take notes during the meeting. In addition, arrangements should be made for community members to submit their concerns, interests, and ideas to the superintendent before the final version of the plan is submitted to the board.

- Consider the oral and written views of school and community people when the long-range plan for achieving excellence is revised.

- Submit the final plan to the board for approval.

- Publicize and promote the plan on a continuous basis.

- Make it a point to do what George Jenkins, founder of the Publix Super Markets, did when he was building his company into one of the best-run companies to work for in America—arrange to take one- and two-week trips annually, traveling the country in search of new ideas.

Support
School Champions

Anyone can be a hero if he has the confidence and persistence to try.
—TERRENCE F. DEAL AND ALAN A. KENNEDY

Peters and Waterman refer to them as champions, Deal and Kennedy refer to them as heros, and I refer to them as prime movers. Whatever title is used to describe them, a school district cannot achieve excellence without them. Champions personify the values of the school organization and epitomize the strength of the organization. They are motivators, emulators, miracle workers, healers, and problem solvers. They are usually the persons who can be counted on to complete a project or to arrive at a creative and viable solution to a problem. They are risk-oriented people who know exactly what they are doing and where they are heading. They at times may seem like troublemakers—playful, obnoxious, innovative, egotistical, impatient, arrogant, somewhat irrational, adamant, persistent, and competitive. As a result, they may not be promoted, recognized, taken seriously, or even rewarded for their efforts. They will resort to experimentation, trial and error, emulation, bootlegging, or outright stealing of another person's idea to achieve their goal.

National Science Foundation studies suggest that a champion's role is crucial in actualizing an idea. Ed Schon of MIT maintains that "a new idea either finds a champion or it dies." Peter Drucker expresses the same sentiments when he says, "Whenever anything is being accomplished, it is being done, I have learned, by a monomaniac with a mission. In the words of Peters and Watermman, "No support systems, no champion; no champions, no innovations." I would like to add to this statement, "No innovations, forget about excellence." Without innovations, our school districts will not be able to keep abreast of changing times and conditions and the needs of our students.

The Types of Champions

School districts must essentially do two things: They must provide a school environment in which champions will emerge, and once they do, they must protect them. The role of the champion is to bring to fruition ideas for improving the present performance of the school district. The role of the protector is to understand the achievements of the champions, to teach other people within the school organization to understand and appreciate champions, and to protect them.

Some school administrators and board members don't understand the importance of champions, and neither are they willing to give them "room" to move the school organization forward. For this reason, school administrators must not only teach board members to understand the importance of school champions, but also execute a plan to create and nurture them. They must understand that school champions are the key to school improvement and that they should be protected and supported. If they are, almost anything is possible.

2

There are three types of champions, as reported by Peters and Waterman:

- The "product champion" is a highly goal oriented person and is a fervent believer in whatever he or she has in mind. Because of a strong desire to bring an idea to fruition, he or she may neglect relatives, friends, and colleagues. The product champion tends to be self-assured, dynamic, and self-confident, and at times pushy and even arrogant.

- The "executive champion" is usually a former product champion who has undergone the hardship of "pushing an idea to fruition" and understands what it takes to do so. The role of this champion is to run interference for teaching product champions. An executive champion tends to be dynamic and goal oriented; he or she often acts as a stroker, a negotiator, or a facilitator.

- The "godfather champion" is a well-seasoned executive champion who serves as the role model for other champions. Because of his or her past experience as a product and executive champion, the godfather champion will provide the necessary support to save champions from themselves as well as to save them from the countless number of others who may resist anything they do. In addition, he or she sets standards of performance, makes excellence attainable, symbolizes the company to others, and induces employees to improve performance.

The types of champions in school districts are basically similar to those in the best-run companies, but with some differences. There are four types of champions that can be created and nurtured in school districts.

- "Teaching champions" are basically teachers who have developed and/or emulated a teaching style that has enabled them to get excellent and sometimes outstanding results from students. They are strong student advocates. They are often used as a model by other teachers. They are highly regarded by parents and students, and misjudged by some teachers, principals, and other administrators. If they don't get adequate support from their principals, they are prone to move on to greener pastures.

- "Program champions" usually are principals, but some teachers as well as central administrators have been known to produce and support a program or product that they strongly believe will produce excellent results for students. Program champions are highly risk oriented and will go to great lengths to push a program or product. They can be pushy, bullheaded, and persistent movers.

- "Executive champions" in public schools tend to be principals, assistant superintendents, and superintendents who have been successful teaching and program champions. They carry out the role of supporter and protector of other school champions by highlighting what those people have achieved and how the school district as a whole has gained from their achievements.

- "Godfather champions" in public schools tend to look for championship traits in school administrators and to act as mentors to both executive and

4

program champions. They tend to be superintendents.

I believe it is appropriate at this time to describe the activities of four school champions who came out of hiding to champion a worthy cause with or without the support of the school district.

George Cureton was a teaching champion who taught first grade in the Newark Public School System. He tried more than a dozen reading programs before he got the idea of relating the phonetic approach to reading to activities that students could relate to. Therefore, instead of teaching his first graders the alphabet, he taught them the sounds of the alphabet by first using concrete articles and then slowly replacing the concrete with the abstract. Students were taught to slide sounds of the alphabet to produce words. For example, the word "mark" would produce "muh-Arthur-kick." He also used certain expressions to get over certain sounds; for example, the "your mama going to get you" sound was the "oo" sound, the doctor sound was the "ah" sound, the punch-in-the-stomach sound was the "uh" sound, etc. He also taught vowels by indicating that when certain letters are separated by a consonant, the first vowel will give its strength to the other vowel, changing the sound of the word. In Cureton's classroom, every student who responded correctly to the lesson was lifted, hugged, kissed, shown off to the class, and given applause by the class. Students who did not respond correctly to a question were given an opportunity to redeem themselves by answering the question later during the lesson. Usually, the class responded to correct answers by these students with thunderous cheers and applause. As a result of this teaching champion's creative efforts, none of his students was ever a nonreader. Usually, the percentage of nonreaders in a first grade class is about 10 to 15 percent. More than 90 percent of George Cureton's

5

students scored above the first grade level, with nearly 60 percent of the students scoring at the third grade level on the Metropolitan Achievement Test. Although George Cureton never got promoted and never received the recognition he rightfully deserved in the system, he did become New Jersey Teacher of the Year in the seventies and later was nominated for Teacher of the Year nationwide. After leaving the Newark School System, he went on to become a professor, but not in education. Yes, we lost a school champion.

John Howarth is a program/executive champion who is superintendent of the Northern Valley Regional High School in New Jersey. In 1983, he became an enthusiast of the quality circle program and attended a five-day intensive and comprehensive facilitator's workshop about the program. Most of the superintendents who attended this workshop implemented the program with their teachers. John Howarth was the exception. He developed his own materials, asked for student volunteers from the student council, requested two teachers to attend eight training sessions which he personally conducted, and created a student quality circle program. The teachers subsequently became the facilitators of the program. The program proved highly successful in solving problems that had existed in the school for years. As a result of this program, some teachers also became interested in the quality circle concept. This program champion forged ahead and established what may have been the first student quality circle program in the nation.

Robert Mastruzzi of John F. Kennedy High School in New York City is an executive champion who gives his staff the kind of support, autonomy, and independence that helps to create and nurture teaching and program champions. He not only protects his staff from policies and procedures that might impede the progress of excellent schools, but often thinks of ways in which he can run interference for his people to provide a support system for those who endeavor to do things for kids. By being tolerant of mistakes, Mastruzzi creates an environment in which people feel free to try again and again, even if they are not successful. This is an ideal environment for encouraging championship behavior.

When I think of godfather champions, I remember an executive school champion who was superintendent of the Cherry Creek School District in Colorado in the latter half of the 1960s. His name is Edwin Pino. Ed Pino created an educational climate in which school people were encouraged and rewarded for finding new and effective ways for educating kids. When I first appeared in Cherry Creek School District to witness what Edwin Pino and his staff were doing, I was very much impressed. It was during the nongraded, individualized instruction and differentiated staffing era. When others were merely talking about these innovations, the Cherry Creek School District was carrying them out. Instead of the textbook, teachermade learning packages were the focal point of learning. Instead of being confined to a specific grade, teachers were grouped in teams and taught multi-graded classes, thereby making the most of their individual strengths and talents. Instead of being required to sign out library books, students were permitted the freedom to take any book home without a library card. Instead of assuming the role of boss, principals served as coaches, facilitators, and protectors of teaching champions.

Peters and Waterman state that the godfather champion "is typically an aging teacher who provides models for championing." Even as an executive school champion way back in the sixties, Edwin Pino was seen by his administrators as a role model. Today he still reigns as one of the truly great school champions, as he travels around the country preaching how to achieve excellence in our schools.

Some school champions have experienced great hardship trying to survive in an organization oblivious of their importance to its success. I shall describe three.

Myrna C. Adams served as an elementary teacher in the Chicago school system about eight years ago. She was highly respected as a teacher by both her peers and her students (and many parents). Her performance record was indeed proof that she was a teaching champion. When most teachers were using exclusively the basic text to teach reading, she supplemented the text with comic books, magazines, and other items that the students could relate to. When her peers assigned seat work to their students and remained at their desks, she was busy wandering around her classroom, talking and listening. When most teachers were rushing to leave the portals of the school, she remained in the building, sometimes until late at night, to assist students with their homework, coach them, and help them in any other way she could. As a result of Ms. Adams's champion-like performance, her kids scored higher on achievement tests than most students. Her students' absentee rate was one of the lowest in the school district.

However, she had one problem: She was a strong advocate for kids. She would often appear late for meetings because she was attending to one or more students who needed her at that moment. Other times, she would verbalize her concern about a policy that she felt was not in the best interests of students. Sometimes, she would ask to go to the superintendent's office to address an edict that was insensitive to teachers. Because Ms. Adams, a mover and a challenger, appeared pushy and self-assured, she never received from the administration the recognition, praise, and award that she rightly deserved. Time after time, she was passed over for promotions when non-teaching champions who did not challenge the system were promoted. Eventually, the system took its toll on this teaching champion. She now serves as a special assistant to the vice-president for student development of Old Westbury College in Old

Westbury, New York. Recently, when Ms. Adams was discussing her teaching stint in Chicago and her experience on the college level, a colleague said to her, "You represent the conscience of the institution and no one likes to hear the conscience." What a shame.

The second unrewarded school champion who comes to mind is a program/executive champion who served as an executive director of a regional service center in New Jersey. He had an outstanding record of exposing school people to innovative principles and practices, was the author of numerous books on innovative practices in education, and had a passion for evaluating training of educators based on student achievement. He was charged by the state department of education with using school resources for personal gain, being anti-Semitic, and stealing the authorship of a book. After this champion displayed more than $14,000 in checks for services received within and outside of the center, demonstrated that his deputy as well as nearly 30 percent of his staff was Jewish, and displayed the certificate of copyright for his book, the grand jury found it proper and fitting not to indict him.

Champions are very conscientious people, but they are constantly grappling with the system and are into anything that might help them realize their vision. Therefore, anyone seeking evidence to bring them up for dismissal or on charges is likely to find some. In most of these cases, the evidence is superficial at most, because the "intent" of almost all champions is honorable: the best interests of kids. Even Edwin Pino, who seemed to be one of the nation's outstanding superintendents and executive champions, began to experience a number of problems when the school board changed hands and his champion-like management style was misjudged for something else. Finally, rather than continue to fight the system, Ed Pino found it fitting to resign his position and seek other ways to champion the cause of excellence in public education.

There are probably hundreds or thousands of similar stories illustrating that our school champions are not supported, are not protected, and are not adored as they are in our best-run companies. We can no longer afford to lose our school champions and must do whatever it takes to create and nurture them.

Some school champions have had more difficulty than others in a school district. Champions usually experience trouble when they start out to realize their vision, but when the champion is black, Hispanic, or female, the difficulty can be almost unbearable. This is because school administrators and other school people in general have a standard notion of how members of these groups should behave, based on either sexism or racism, and when their behavior is glowingly outside these preconceived norms, problems are likely to erupt. Many people have great difficulty tolerating white male champions who may be arrogant, egotistical, bullheaded, etc. When a champion happens to be black, Hispanic, or female, many people will not even make an attempt. The point I wish to make is that school administrators may have to work harder to accept and to support school champions who are from a minority group.

Supporting School Champions

How can school districts support champions? They can take a lesson from the best-run companies: Break up schools and other units into more manageable entities, teams consisting of eight to ten people who work together either on a permanent basis or until a project is completed. For example, Texas Instruments has 9,000 temporary teams that solve job-related problems. Sometimes innovative products and techniques spring from the efforts of these teams. More is said in Lessons 11 and 12 about dividing into teams and giving teachers and other school people a great deal of autonomy. Teams that can work autonomously are free to find clever and innovative ways to improve instruction for students. Most of the best-run companies have provided various degrees of autonomy to divisions and other units, and this autonomy has resulted in numerous innovative projects.

IBM, Digital, and Raychem have instituted what they refer to as limited autonomy, in which salespersons are also problem-solvers. This technique can be applied in public education by encouraging teaching champions or teaching fellows to go directly to the kids to find out about problems with instruction, for example. Some teachers and principals think this is a form of snooping, but if the teachers are not penalized but helped to improve the instructional process they will begin to accept the technique. Making this method work will involve convincing school champions or teaching fellows that they are champions and are much admired by the school district. Some readers may say that this will be debilitating to the morale of the rest of the school people, but this is not necessarily the case, particularly if there is a commitment to build trust in the school district.

The best-run companies have found that internal competition through teams has had the effect of bringing out the champion in people. For example, brand teams compete with each other at Procter & Gamble. Duplication and overlapping have also been permitted in order to bring out champions at Digital, Hewlett-Packard, and Johnson & Johnson, to mention just a few companies. In schools, internal competition could take the form of joint student and teacher contests, in which the teams and students with the highest attendance, for example, win a reward. Before long, emerging champions would develop creative and innovative ways within their teams to beat their competition. There also could be competition for the best teaching method, the best technique to maintain classroom discipline, etc.

Another way to support champions is by intensifying the communication process so that they have an opportunity to assert themselves. For example, at 3M, there are countless numbers of unscheduled meetings of people and teams to discuss and solve problems. At Digital, the CEO sees his role as a catalyst or devil's advocate. As a result, he has frequent meetings with engineering committees from all levels of the company to discuss problems and what can be done to deal with them. There is reason to believe that a championing system works best when there is a great deal of informal interaction and a *de facto* informal culture. I see no reason why the superintendent of schools cannot meet with department people to share ideas and discuss problems. This could also be done with students, with teaching champions or fellows in attendance. Intel has a process called "decision making by peers" in which open, blunt, confrontation-oriented meetings are used to iron out differences and to discuss reasons for problems and solutions to them. School administrators could only implement this type of meeting if they were honest with themselves and felt secure that what they said would not be used to punish or penalize them in the future. I believe that introducing seminars in which each building principal has to discuss the progress or lack of progress of his or her particular school with peers would be an ideal way to emulate Intel's decision making by peers program and would provide opportunities for program and executive champions to offer their ideas for achieving excellence.

At IBM, a "fellow" program has been organized whereby fellows are given virtually free rein for five years to shake up the system. A fellow can see a problem, have an idea as to how it could be solved, and request assistance in solving the problem from other people within the company. When the problem has been solved, the fellow reports on the problem and solution to management, which then puts the necessary activities together to move the company forward. This type of fellow program could work in a school district. Many may think retaining a large number of fellows would be too costly, but one to three fellows could perhaps do more for the school district in terms of achieving excellence than the most expensive program. A careful screening process must be put in motion to identify the most likely candidates for this fellow program. These persons could very well be the teaching champions or program champions mentioned previously. These fellows would have one charge: to search for problems in the school district and to solve them. They would be given two to three years to achieve this feat.

3M has what is known as the Venture Team, which is a task force of employees from various disciplines who voluntarily organize to solve a company problem. These teams are similar to quality circles, except that instead of working on a multitude of unit-related problems, they work on a single product that may result in a new and profitable venture for the company or a crucial area of the organization. How could these venture teams be employed in school districts? Let's say the superintendent has a very important major project which he or she wants a task force to tackle, such as determining how to give teachers more autonomy in their building. Instead of being identified as a new venture team, the team could be called the important project team (IPT) or new project team. All of the team members would be volunteers, who would be assigned to the project on a full-time basis. Such a team should consist of a cross-section of professional people and have one specific charge (for example: to develop a comprehensive plan for providing more autonomy for teachers while at the same time preserving the self-esteem of the building administration in an endeavor to achieve excellence in teaching and learning). The important project team's task the first year would be to develop the plan. Its task the second year would be to implement the plan. As the programs grew and prospered, champions would benefit by getting promoted and seeing the fruits of their labor.

There are other techniques used by the best-run companies to support champions. 3M uses executive champions to protect young champions from premature intrusions from headquarters staff and to move them out of the line of fire. At 3M, the executive champion is a coach and a mentor. He or she must have a great deal of patience and skill in developing other champions. Although executive champions must be tolerant of mistakes, they must also bring mistakes to the attention of school personnel so that others will learn and grow from them.

Publix Super Market has a policy of benign neglect by which each store manager is given a great deal of autonomy to operate a store in his or her own fashion. As a result of this practice, champions are allowed to submerge themselves in their projects and are supported by headquarters.

IBM shows off its champions. For example, in one edition of the company newsletter "Think," IBM publicizes the accomplishment of one of its salesmen, who for over thirty years was a member of the company's Hundred Percent Club. By showing off this champion, IBM was saying, in effect, here is a champion to emulate.

3M gives its scientists and engineers free time to become champions. During that time, they can work on any of their personal projects.

How to Nurture School Champions

There are a number of ways in which school administrators can create and nurture champions. The following represent some of them:

- Remove obstacles that impede the progress of champions. These obstacles can take the form of policies and procedures of the central administration office, a verbal order from the superintendent, or an act of an individual or group of people who may not be sympathetic to the quest for excellence by champions. This means that at times the executive champion must have the guts to assume risks and allow the teaching and program champions to bend the rules, and in some cases even to break them.

- Tolerate champions even if they are a nuisance. Remember, champions can be arrogant, egotistical, bullheaded, and determined to do things their own way to reach their goal, even at considerable risk. Other people must be aware of the traits and characteristics of champions and allow them the space to be themselves.

- Tolerate and nurture failure. Champions will not always be successful. In fact, they will probably fail more times than they will succeed. The important thing is to recognize that unless school administrators are tolerant of mistakes and failures, champions and emerging champions will not rise above the crowd. Peters and Waterman maintain that "tolerance for failure is a very specific part of the excellent company culture, and lessons come directly from the top." One of the chief duties of the executive champion is to run interference for teaching and program champions when they make a blunder, by sticking up for them and by educating other school and community people as to their value to the school district.

- Become knowledgeable about the traits and characteristics of champions and be alert to stories about high risk-oriented achievers who tend to behave differently from the rest of the school people.

- Request that principals identify their champions and potential champions and prepare a plan for creating and/or nurturing them.

- Conduct a full-day seminar on "creating and nurturing champions." Invite school champions to participate in this seminar to discuss their activities and accomplishments with participants.

- Put champions on a high pedestal.

- Disseminate a newsletter explaining the various activities of champions and their impact on the school district. Be certain to include general articles on "How anyone can become a champion."

- Become a strong advocate of experimentation and innovation and let everybody know it.

- Identify an important school district need and then search out a champion who is willing to find a solution to that need. Publicize the case from beginning to end.

- Put champions in charge of important projects and task forces.

- Maintain weekly contact with all champions to see what they are doing and offer assistance and, upon returning to the office, jot down any followup activities you can contribute.

- Provide opportunities for champions to receive recognition, praise, awards, and rewards. Champions enjoy hoopla. An effective support system to create and nurture champions includes an assortment of activities to celebrate their achievements. These celebrations will demonstrate to both champions and other school people that champions are looked upon with high esteem. The result, the acceptance and appreciation of champions, will gradually become a well-documented value of the school organization. The reward for champions should have a dual effect. It should provide the champion with an individual incentive to keep up championship efforts, and it should enable the people who are affected and enjoy the rewards to give credit where due.

Be Cautious of Some Community Champions

Although school champions are to be admired and cherished, there is a type of self-proclaimed community champion who should be closely observed, particularly if that person is a member of the board of education. I am aware of one self-proclaimed community champion who is probably doing more harm to the kids of that district than the worst teacher. She made herself a champion of the people (she has actually been called a godmother) by organizing committees to deliver food and clothing to the needy, by distributing toys to kids at Christmas time, by contacting certain influential persons to do favors for community people, by getting jobs for her people within and outside the school district, by getting school administrators to give banquets for her, by championing the causes of ineffectual school administrators, and by playing a direct role in ousting at least one superintendent and other school administrators who disagreed with her. Whenever incompetent school people have a problem with the administration, they will go straight to the godmother and she will "fix things."

Because this board member has a high need for self-esteem, everything else must take a back seat, even the education of the students. I have had an opportunity to observe this board member on numerous occasions at board meetings. She will spend a minimum of time on matters directly related to the education of students and a great deal of time defending incompetence and mediocrity, or getting job slots filled only by her people. When I queried an administrator about this, he merely looked at me and shook his head in shame. One cannot support incompetence and achieve excellence. A school board that does nothing to expose and combat misdirected board members is just as guilty as the misdirected member. As one community member says, "The community gets what it deserves." How true, however unfortunate in some cases.

Strategies for Achieving Excellence

A school district administrator can take the following steps to help champions to blossom:

- First, identify school champions by making a set of four lists. Go to principals and ask them to identify all of the outstanding teachers in their buildings. Make a list of these teachers. Then go to the teachers on that list and ask them to identify the outstanding teachers, and put these on a second list. Make a third list of teachers who appear on both lists. Interview all of the teachers on the third list to determine if any of them have high risk-oriented hobbies such as skydiving, rock climbing, or hang gliding. Put these teachers on the fourth list. These are either school champions or potential school champions.

- Next, arrange to meet with the people on the fourth list individually to interview them with regard to their needs. Develop a series of questions designed to determine what their individual needs are and how the principal, the supervisor, the superintendent, and the school district as a whole can help them to fulfill their needs. (This questionnaire should perhaps be developed by the human resources or personnel department with input from other school people.) Some training may be needed to teach the interviewers how to administer the questionnaire. Once the results have been collected and thoroughly analyzed, a report should be prepared and used as a foundation for "letting loose those champions." However, before implementing such a plan, do an old quality circle trick: Call in an expert or a highly regarded professional to verify the soundness of the implementation plan. I have found that when a plan has been verified prior to implementation, it stands a better chance of achieving success. Another useful technique is to invite the champions into the meeting with the experts in an effort to gain their input too. Some school districts may wish to invite the experts to verify the plan after a separate meeting has been conducted with the group of champions.

19

- Once the plan has been verified and approved by the board, set it in motion. After a short period of time, say maybe six months, individual champions should be interviewed to determine how well their needs are being met.

Some educators may feel that champion groups will become an elite class of people and will be resented by other school people. This probably will be true to some extent. Informing school people of the results helps to minimize resentment, as does the fact that champions usually confine their activities to their own units and rarely get together as a full group to establish the sort of fraternal organization that arouses jealousy. I am of the belief that even if a few school people were to "generate negative energy" about champions, this would not be harmful to the harmony of the school district. It would only imply that the executive champion had more work to do to convince the "bad mouthers" of the importance of champions to the success of the school district.

Adopt a Suggestion Program

Training organizes . . . mind power and experience. The
suggestion box . . . collects the ideas.

—CLAIR F. VOUGH

Employee suggestion programs have been operating successfully in industry since the turn of the century. Eastman Kodak established the first employee suggestion program in the United States in 1898. Under this program, if a suggestion saves the company money, the award is equal to 15 percent of the savings achieved in the first two years of use; if the suggestion results in a new product, the award is equal to 3 percent of the first year of annual sales. In recent years Kodak has given, on the average, $1.6 million a year to 9,550 employees who have offered ideas. And since the program's inception, Kodak has adopted more than 700,000 ideas submitted by its employees, who have received more than $120 million in return.

At IBM, in 1983 six employees were awarded $100,000 each for cost-saving ideas that helped to improve IBM operations. The awards, which were the maximum provided under IBM's employee suggestion program, were part of approximately $14 million awarded that year for some 36,000 suggestions which altogether saved the company at least $65 million. The suggestion program was even more successful in 1984. During that year IBM employees earned approximately $17 million in awards for ideas that resulted in savings of more than $100 million, or an increase of $35 million over 1983.

At Marion Laboratories, the Marion Spirit Suggestion Awards Program provides for stock to be given to associates (employees) who generate money-saving suggestions. In 1982 the company gave stock valued at $15,000, $12,000, and $7,000 to three associates for accepted suggestions. In addition, each year the person who offers the best suggestion(s) receives a week-long, all-expenses-paid trip for two to any city in the world, as well as an extra week of vacation.

General Motors is the largest employer in the United States to have a suggestion program. With approximately 500,000 employees eligible to participate, in 1984 about 290,000 employees submitted suggestions and more than $34 million has been awarded to 104,000 employees whose suggestions were accepted.

A model suggestion program that deserves mention is the one used by Maytag. The program, called "Work Simplification," went into effect in 1947. There are three stages in this program. First, all employees and supervisors are required to attend training sessions on simplifying work. Second, any employee with a suggestion must fill out a two-page form in which he or she describes the idea(s) and gives an estimate of how much money and time the idea could save the company. Third, the employee reviews this form with his or her supervisor, and together they attempt to improve on the suggestion before submission. Employees whose ideas are accepted receive one half of the savings realized over the first six months of the idea's implementation up to a maximum of $5,000. Supervisors are not compensated for their contributions to the suggestions, but are honored at an annual banquet. In 1982, 1,529 Maytag employees, or 53 percent of those eligible, submitted 5,007 suggestions (an average of 3.2 suggestions per employee), and approximately 2,400 of these were implemented. Implementation cost the company $141,284 but resulted in savings of more than $4.5 million, or nearly 32 times the expenditure for the program. Since its inception, Maytag's program has won top honors in twelve of the past thirteen years from the National Association of Suggestion Systems for its exceptional success. Usually a company can expect to receive an average of 225 suggestions per year for every 1,000 eligible employees, and about 25 percent of these suggestions will be acceptable. Savings for the company are usually five to ten times greater than the expenditures for implementing the program.

Most of the best-managed companies in Japan have been quick to capitalize on their own version of the employee suggestion program. For example, in one year at Matsushita Electric Company, 6,500 employees generated 85,000 suggestions; these figures translate into 233 suggestions a day or more than one suggestion a month for each employee. One of the most successful suggestion programs in the world is that of Toyota of Japan. Nine hundred thousand suggestions are generated each year by Toyota employees or an average of 20 per employee, and these result in savings for the company of nearly a quarter of a billion dollars.

School Districts Have Been Slow to Act

Although the first suggestion program was adopted in this country almost ninety years ago, school districts have only recently shown an interest in generating ideas from school people. In fact, in the National Association of Suggestion Systems, only about twelve of the more than 1,000 organizations represent school districts, or little more than 1 percent. You would think that large school districts, like large companies such as IBM, Maytag, and General Motors, would be members of the association, but this is not the case.

Of course, some readers may point out that for years the Chicago School District maintained a suggestion box in the office of the superintendent. This is true, but such a suggestion "program" merely elicits complaints and what I call small suggestions that generally don't have much impact. A genuine suggestion program has a well-conceived plan and is backed by money and other kinds of awards. It is not used to receive employees' complaints.

Why haven't school districts implemented suggestion programs?

- Too few superintendents are fully knowledgeable about the positive impact of a suggestion program.

- Some superintendents are not cost conscious.

- Until recently many school officials did not view profit-making companies as fitting examples for school districts.

- Many school administrators have had little faith in the ideas and opinions of non-decision makers.

- Finally, superintendents tend to shy away from any plans involving cash awards because of possible negative community reaction.

There is nothing illegal about a board of education's adopting a suggestion program and awarding cash payments to individuals or teams. After all, if merit pay can be awarded to individual teachers for achieving excellence, an individual or team should be able to receive a monetary award for suggesting an idea that will help a school district achieve excellence. If for some reason public funds cannot be used to support an employee suggestion program, a school administrator who is committed to the suggestion program can come up with creative ideas for raising outside funds to support the program. He or she could ask the Parent-Teacher Association to raise funds for the program, could get local industry to contribute funds, or could request that a community group sponsor the program. If the benefits of the suggestion are explained to the community in an effective manner, there should be very little negative feeling about the program. It is interesting to note that in the three school districts in which I interviewed those in charge of the suggestion program, it was a community member or a group that had recommended to school officials the adoption of a suggestion program.

Establishing a School Suggestion Program

Basically, an individual or team suggestion program is a formalized procedure established by the superintendent to solicit from school employees suggestions and ideas that will have a significant and positive impact on the school district, and to award those whose suggestions are accepted. Suggestion programs tend to improve employee relations, involve those closest to the problems in coming up with solutions, generate numerous ideas for improving the school organization, and enhance school district morale.

In order for a school suggestion program to produce these positive results, it must be supported by the school environment. First, the superintendent must understand the advantages of a suggestion program and feel that there is a real need for it. Second, the program must not be implemented in isolation but must be an outgrowth of the philosophy and purposes of the school organization. And finally, expected results of the suggestion program must be stated in board policy and must be made clear to all school people.

A school suggestion program should be established not merely to save money but also to improve students' learning and growth. In fact I maintain that if at least 50 percent of the suggestions do not directly concern teaching, this suggests in and of itself that certain areas of the school district are in need of change. Those areas most likely to be in need of change would be teacher training and development and management of the instructional process. I cannot overemphasize this point. Training plus experience equals suggestions. If teachers are not provided with continuous training and with opportunities to plan, manage and teach, their experiences will be limited and so will their suggestions.

Following are a number of recommendations for establishing an employee suggestion program:

- Establish the budget for the suggestion program, drawing on the general funds and/or contributions received from vendors and local community businesses and associations.

- Determine the composition and functions of the suggestion program committee.

- Outline for the committee the questions that have to be addressed in establishing a program. Among the questions:

   - Who will be eligible and ineligible to participate in the program?
   - By what means will suggestions be submitted— i.e., a suggestion box, suggestion inspectors, or suggestion secretaries?
   - What procedures will be followed in accepting and rejecting suggestions?
   - How can rejections be handled in a humane manner? (A procedure should exist for indicating the reason for each rejection).

- Determine possible areas that suggestions might address in order to be considered for an award. In school suggestion programs these areas are:

  - Improvement in student learning and growth
  - Improvement in service to students
  - Improvement in working conditions
  - Improvement in methods, techniques, and procedures
  - Reduction or prevention of waste
  - Improvement of tools, machines, or equipment
  - Improvement in handling methods
  - Reduction in time
  - Reduction or elimination of unnecessary procedures, paperwork, materials, equipment, and so forth
  - Other cost saving ideas.

- Determine the nature of the award. Keep in mind that monetary awards greatly increase the success of a suggestion program. If monetary awards are used, one approach would be to have the amount awarded equal to 10 percent of the money saved by the suggestion. If the improvement was not a financial one—say a team of teachers made a suggestion that increased the average median growth of students in math — the award might equal 10 percent of the sum of the teachers' salaries and be equally divided among them. It is highly recommended that awards be provided on both an individual and a team basis, especially if teamwork is something the school district would like to foster. Some of America's best-run companies have found that a team suggestion program can be extremely successful even when an individual suggestion program has not achieved what was expected.

The experiences of the school districts that I have conferred with indicate that a $200 award is not a strong enough incentive. I would recommend awards in the vicinity of $1,000.

- Create the proper environment for a successful suggestion program: give teachers the freedom to be creative, provide them with examples of some suggestions that have saved money and of some that have increased students' learning and growth, and offer them more opportunities for training and visitation.

- Have a central administrator or a committee develop a comprehensive plan for implementing the suggestion program.

- Select someone to oversee the program. Usually this person will be the assistant superintendent for human resources or personnel. Cite all of the person's functions and responsibilities, including the development of a marketing strategy to promote the suggestion program on a continuous basis.

Strategies for Achieving Excellence

- Become a member of the National Association of Suggestion Systems, located at 230 North Michigan Avenue, Suite 1200, Chicago, IL 60601; (312) 372-1770. Membership and initiation fees are $150. By becoming a member of this association you will be eligible to receive materials pertaining to other suggestion programs. You will also automatically receive their newsletter.

- By means of the association's membership list, contact other school districts that are in the process of adopting a suggestion program or have already done so and discuss with them their experiences.

- Contact those companies that have been recognized by the association as outstanding in order to acquire their materials, ideas, and recommendations.

- Implement Lessons 3 and 7, either concommitantly with or prior to the adoption of the program. One of the reasons Maytag's suggestion program is highly acclaimed is because training in work simplification is part of the suggestion program.

- "Talk up and write up" the impact of the program by publicizing the number of suggestions submitted, the number accepted, the names of individuals and/or teams submitting accepted suggestions, the cost of implementing any suggestions, and the positive results achieved through implemented suggestions. For example, you might submit a news release entitled "School district's suggestion program improves student achievement and saves taxpayers' money."

- Evaluate the schools in your district by the number of suggestions generated. If the results fall below an expected figure, such as one per month per school employee, conduct a study to determine the reasons and initiate an appropriate corrective actions.

- In order to stimulate new ideas, circulate on a consistent basis books and articles on innovative programs and activities implemented by other school districts.

- Send an article on how to improve productivity or achieve excellence in schools to all school administrators, supervisors, and selected teachers, along with a memo asking that they read the article and reply with written comments on how to improve productivity or achieve excellence in school. Publish the results and initiate appropriate action. Forward a letter of thanks to all of the respondents.

- Consider adopting—but only after the employee suggestion program is operating smoothly—a student and community suggestion program whereby students and community people can generate suggestions and receive awards.

- Remember: A suggestion program that does not offer money among other awards will be extremely limited in effectiveness. A team suggestion program is more effective than an individual suggestion program. And the strength of a suggestion program is based on the training and development opportunities and varied experiences of those participating in the program.

• LESSON 3 •

Move from Philosophy to Culture

Culture building requires renewed application of some "soft" management skills, but that doesn't mean it's a simple or easy matter.
—CRAIG R. HICKMAN AND MICHAEL A. SILVA

A prevailing problem in far too many school districts in this country—a problem that keeps them from achieving excellence—is that school people do not know what is expected of them. In other words, they go about performing their jobs with no set of macroprinciples and guidelines.

Why does this situation exist?

In some cases, the school district has never even bothered to articulate its values or set forth a philosophy. This is an essential first step if people within the district are to understand how they should act and why.

What happens in more cases, however, is that a statement of philosophy does exist, but school people are barely familiar with it and are not acting in accordance with the principles and guidelines it sets forth. In such cases we say that the philosophy has not been inculcated into the patterns of behavior or "culture" of the school district.

There are several reasons why this situation occurs with such frequency. First, in many school districts the district's philosophy has been formulated not by a committee of school personnel and community members but by a single person—such as the person hired to develop the school district's pol-

31

icy manual, or the assistant superintendent of curriculum and instruction, or the superintendent himself or herself. As a result, the philosophy is not widely known or accepted as representing the views or values of people in the district. Second, too many superintendents have failed to make the connection between the philosophy and the culture of the school district. For some strange reason they feel that the culture will take care of itself once the philosophy has been formulated. Third, most superintendents have not received proper graduate training in how to inculcate a professed philosophy within a school district. Therefore, very little occurs in this area. Fourth, the agencies evaluating our schools have placed more emphasis on whether or not a philosophy exists than on whether or not the philosophy is expressed in the culture. Education officials have much to learn in this crucial area.

Formulating a Philosophy

If your school district does not have a statement or philosophy, one should be written. If it does have one but the statement has not been updated recently by a committee of school people and community members, I strongly recommend that a new one be formulated from the beginning.

Before the philosophy can be written, however, a decision has to be made as to what elements it will contain. In my opinion, a statement of philosophy should consist of a description of the district's socio-economic purposes, a shared values statement, and discussions of the district's mission, organizational properties, and organizational objectives. If I were asked to identify those elements of the statement of philosophy that are absolutely essential, I would cite the mission and the shared values statements. In determining which elements to include in your district's statement, a review of the elements in the philosophies of some of the best-run companies might help. I therefore suggest that contact be made with Johnson & Johnson to obtain a copy of its socio-economic purposes statement, Apple Computer for its shared values statement, Marion Laboratories for its mission statement, and Rolm Corporation for its corporate properties statement.

The statement of philosophy should be formulated by a committee consisting of a cross-section of school people and community members. It may be best for this committee to meet during the summer, away from the school district. In formulating the philosophy, the committee should work through four stages or steps: the interaction process, the problem-solving phase, the actual writing, and the reaching of a consensus on the final document. Some companies have found it helpful to hire a consultant or facilitator to assist the committee in its work.

The most important phase prior to the actual writing of the philosophy is the interaction phase, which may or may not become heated at times because of the differences in certain norms and values. I maintain that the more interaction that takes place during preparation of the document, the better the quality of the document. Sometimes the nominal group process is used to facilitate the interaction phase. The nominal group process is similar to brainstorming. An essential difference is that instead of vocalizing their initial ideas to a problem, participants write them on cards, after which they are written on a board so that all can see them. Then the interaction takes place.

To begin the interaction process on the shared values statement, the committee may want to use the twelve cultural norms that Saphier and King have pinpointed as positively affecting school improvement. These norms are

- Collegiality
- Experimentation

33

- High expectations

- Trust and confidence

- Tangible support

- Reaching out to the knowledge bases

- Appreciation and recognition

- Caring, celebration, and honor

- Involvement in decision making

- Protection of what's important

- Traditions

- Honest, open communications

In addition to the above, the reader may also like to consider the following:

- Teamwork

- Excellence

- Participative management

- Community participation

- Achievement orientation

- Semi-autonomy

- Intrapreneurship

Inculcating a Philosophy

Once a school district's statement of philosophy has been approved by the board of education, the question becomes

How can the philosophy be inculcated into the district's culture?

It would seem that the essential first step, which is the job of the superintendent, is to see that the district's philosophy is reflected in its policies and operations. A close congruence of philosophy and operations is characteristic of the best-run companies. Consider, for example, Hewlett-Packard and Advanced Micro Devices.

Hewlett-Packard's philosophy, called the HP Way, incorporates the following principles and commitments:

- Belief in people; freedom

- Respect and dignity; individual self-esteem

- Recognition; sense of achievement; participation

- Security; performance; development of people

- Insurance; personal worry protection

- Sharing of benefits and responsibility; mutual help

- MBO; decentralization

- Informality, open communication

- A chance to learn by making mistakes

- Training and education; counseling

- Performance and enthusiasm

Is Hewlett-Packard's statement of philosophy reflected in its actions? To answer this question, let's explore one set of principles and commitments contained in the HP Way: "security; performance; development of people." Hewlett-Packard has an unwritten policy of not laying off employees even during difficult times and to this day remains one of the dozen or so best-run companies that has not laid off a single employee. The company also provides numerous opportunities for employees to participate in not only vertical but also horizontal training activities in order to expand their growth and development and to make themselves more qualified to seek promotions from within the organization. So it does appear that at least in this case the principles set out in the HP Way are being practiced by the company.

As part of its philosophy, Advanced Micro Devices maintains that "growth means opportunity, both for the company and for AMD's people, and that how we grow is as important as growth itself. So, we have committed ourselves to excellence in everything we do, believing that excellence will spawn growth and opportunity for all of us. From this philosophy has evolved a set of commitments or pillars which underlie our growth to date and provide the platform for continued growth:

- A commitment to our people—people first, products and profits will follow.

- A commitment to innovation—win by out-innovating the competition.

- A commitment to quality—the American Champion of quality products.

- A commitment to our customers—most customer-oriented company in the industry."

Is AMD's philosophy reflected in its actions? As far as its commitment to its people is concerned, a manager of product control had this to say: "I'm proud of our company, especially when I see other companies laying off their employees during a recession, and then Jerry Sanders [AMD president] appears on the *Phil Donahue Show* telling the world he refuses to do that to his people."

The company's commitment to innovation also appears to be a reality. In 1984 Jerry Sanders reported that ". . . last year we introduced 45 new products. This year we plan to introduce 56 new products. . . ." And in reference to the company's commitment to quality, a company controller at AMD said, "The reason AMD's commitment to quality has consistently been met is that we have quality people to meet it. We strive to put the best people in every area of the company, whether it be production, engineering, or finance. When the best people are doing their best work, you can't help but end up with a first-rate product."

This commitment to quality was also confirmed by one of the company's area sales managers, who maintained, "Quality is everything to AMD's European customers. If a quality problem appears in the United States, it is fairly easy to solve. But in Europe, you not only have the problem itself to deal with, you have borders to recross, customs regulations to meet, and language barriers to deal with. All of this can add weeks to the time that it takes to solve a customer's complaints. Before long, you don't have a customer anymore. . . . AMD has pretty well surmounted all of these problems with one thing—its commitment to quality. As a result we have far fewer problems and far more happy customers."

Let's assume that, like those of Hewlett-Packard and Advanced Micro Devices, the school district's policies and practices do conform to its philosophy. As mentioned previously, this is just the first step. A powerful and all-important example has been set, but now the district must initiate a multitude of activities designed to modify and/or change school people's behavior and attitudes to conform to the standards and values espoused in the philosophy. The best-run companies have engaged in an assortment of such activities, and school districts will find many of them helpful. Foremost among these activities is training. In school districts this should be one of the main jobs of principals. One way that such training could be done is through a long-range training program (one conducted over two to three years) that consists of monthly sessions lasting from twenty to thirty minutes. Following are some suggestions as to training activities that could be conducted during these sessions.

Self-indoctrination. Request that each member of a team become familiar with an essential point of one of the elements of the philosophy and then give a ten- to fifteen-minute presentation demonstrating how this particular detail of the philosophy has been realized in the district.

Using Sentence Stems. After the principal explains an element of the statement of philosophy, he or she asks a team member to respond to the explanation by using as a starting point any one of the following sentence stems:
"I believe the mission is . . ."
"I don't believe that our mission is . . . because . . ."
"Our principal does not practice what he (she) preaches because . . ."

Responding to Vignettes. The principal introduces this activity by initiating a discussion about an element of the philosophy. After that, a specific situation or vignette is described and each team member is requested to write a brief description of how he or she would act in that situation in accordance with the philosophy. Team members then divide into mini-teams of three to discuss their responses and to determine which of the three is the best. After ten to fifteen minutes, the entire group reconvenes to discuss each mini-team's decision and to reach a consensus on the most desirable course of action. The original situation presented by the principal should be based on an actual condition existing in the school. The principal can capitalize on this activity by referring the best proposal to the superintendent for consideration.

Sharing the Philosophy. The principal has team members get other team members to focus on the philosophy and have them identify or cite situations in which someone abides by an element of the philosophy.

Guess What Elements. The principal identifies and explains each element of the statement of philosophy. An excerpt from one of the elements is then recited to the team, and team members are requested to identify the element. Sometimes a list of the elements is posted so that the team members can refer to it before responding. If a correct response is given, positive recognition is given and the respondent is asked to elaborate on the response. If an incorrect answer is given, the principal asks the team whether the response was correct and then seeks an answer from another individual.

Response Questions. The principal provides team members with a worksheet containing a series of brief statements about an element of the philosophy. Members complete the worksheet on an individual basis, responding to each statement by indicating whether they strongly agree, agree somewhat, disagree somewhat, or strongly disagree. After that, the team is divided into mini-teams of three who share and discuss their individual responses.

Team-Principal Assessment. The principal sits on a chair in the center of a circle composed of team members. Each individual team member gets a chance to cite five ways in which that principal abides by the philosophy of the school district. After all the members have had a chance to speak, they are each asked to cite five ways in which the principal has not abided by the philosophy. One team member is selected to record the substance of the recitations, and this record is given to the principal at the conclusion of the activity. This activity is not for the weak of heart and should not be used by principals who are timid or do not wish to improve their performance.

In addition to training, a school district should undertake other activities to inculcate its philosophies. Following are some suggested activities based on methods used in the best-run companies:

- Develop a school slogan. Although the mission is usually used as a basis for the school district's slogan, any element of the statement of philosophy can be used for this purpose. Some examples of slogans are as follows:

  –We Are on the Path to Excellence
  –Excellence in Execution

  To inculcate the slogan, print signs that effectively display the slogan and have them posted throughout the school district, refer to the slogan during meetings with school personnel, use the slogan on stationery and other important documents.

- Use employee orientation. Many of the best-run companies introduce their philosophy to new employees during the orientation process.

- Act as a role model. If the words, actions, and deeds of school administrators are consistent with the norms and values of the school district, a strong culture will result; if not, a weak culture will be evident. Role modeling can also be demonstrated through written documents, as well as through the use of the audiovisual aids provided by the training department. In addition, I have found it useful to have school administrators present skits in which they assume roles to demonstrate various aspects and stages of the philosophy.

- Recognize philosophy compliance. Praise school administrators and other school people who are seen practicing a desired value or norm; if their deed has a significant positive effect on the behavior of other school people, give that person an award. In some companies, individuals or teams that exemplify the philosophy are given gift certificates which can be exchanged for merchandise at a store, membership in a health spa, a number of Mondays or Fridays off, or free lunches served by school administrators.

- Communicate the philosophy through written materials. For example, prepare a philosophy manual that describes all of the essential elements of the philosophy; such a manual is invaluable for orientation and career development activities. Some companies also produce newsletters to help spread the gospel of their philosophy; others produce "white papers" and essays, which are distributed among employees and used as the basis for their discussions.

Following is a questionnaire for school administrators based on one developed by Polaroid to elicit from its managers their views of the company's culture.

- What have been the major turning points that have occurred in the school district since its inception?

- What specific and distinctive competencies does the school possess?

- List five phrases or adjectives that best describe the school district.

- What is the best thing that has occurred in the school district within the past two years? The worst?

- Is the culture of the school district collaborative and supportive or individualistic and nonsupportive?

- Are school administration/school people relationships paternalistic or egalitarian?

- To what degree is the school district open or closed to new ideas and suggestions?

- Does the district engage in long-range planning or is it merely reactive and crisis oriented?

- To what degree are school people encouraged to assume risk and not penalized for making mistakes?

- To what extent is the school district willing to engage in a critical self-assessment or to question certain basic assumptions by which it is managed?

- Are new ideas carefully considered and implemented when possible or quickly forgotten because of a lack of commitment on the part of the appropriate staff or committee?

- To what degree is the philosophy of the school district realistic and action oriented or unrealistic and hard to realize?

- To what extent are school people recognized and rewarded for their performance efforts?

- Are the performances of school people rated according to specific results or according to undefined criteria?

Strategies for Achieving Excellence

- Do what Johnson & Johnson does yearly. Involve all central administrators in a Credo Challenge Meeting, where a critical review of each value outlined in the school district's shared value statement is undertaken to determine the extent to which the values are "alive" in the culture of the school district, and what should be done if they are not.

- Organize an all-day "values" conference to be attended by all school personnel. During this conference the attendees should break up into 10- to 12-member groups to discuss whether the values of the school district are "dead" or "alive." Notes should be taken by each team leader on dead values and recommendations made to put life into them. After the conference, every attendee should be given a report that shares the results of the conference and indicates what steps will be taken to put new breath into dead values. Use the substance of the report to prepare a comprehensive three-to- five-day training program for all school administrators to help them revitalize the dead values.

- Consider developing a philosophy around a few central tenets, or "pillars." For example, Conant Associates' philosophy has been erected on four pillars: a problem-solving orientation, intensity of effort, mutual trust and respect among all levels of employees, and exceptional commitment to helping an employee solve his or her personal problems.

- Send for a copy of Advanced Micro Devices' statement of philosophy, and use this as a guide in producing one for your school district.

- Take a cue from Apple Computer—use the shared values statement as an instrument to determine whether or not a job applicant's personality and beliefs are consonant with the values of the school district.

- Retain a marketing firm to develop a high-quality audiovisual presentation of the school district's philosophy for public relations as well as recruitment, orientation, and training purposes. During the development of this presentation, it will be necessary for members of the committee that formulated the philosophy to make sure that the presentation accurately portrays the district's desired philosophy.

- Periodically assess the school district's culture to determine if there are any gaps between desired and existing norms and values. The desired norms and values of course come from the statement of philosophy. To determine existing norms and values, school people could be interviewed and/or sent a questionnaire, or an outside consultant or a committee could conduct a cultural audit by critically examining the following areas:

  –Performance standards and practices
  –Communication flow

–Goals and objectives
–Strategies
–Teampersonship
–Leadership styles and practices
–Student services
–Training and development
–Research and development efforts
–Performance evaluation practices
–Peer relationships
–Innovation practices
–School pride
–Productivity and quality service
–Relationship with stakeholders and community

Once cultural gaps have been identified, they should be ranked in order of importance and appropriate improvement strategies determined. For long-term strategies major emphasis should be placed on role modeling and training. Then an individual or department should be designated to develop a plan for implementing the improvement strategies. This plan should be put into action as soon as possible.

• Have a task force determine whether your district's education strategy matches the culture.

• If the philosophy is not sufficiently inculcated in a particular school, assist the principal in developing a comprehensive and appropriate action plan to improve the culture. Conduct a culture audit prior to and after implementation of the plan for performance evaluation purposes.

Intensify
and Personalize
Communications

The barrier to upward communication, that is often
greater than it need be, is the lack of opportunities . . .
for employees to say what they are thinking and feeling.
—ROSEMARY STEWART

Formal Communications

Information is transmitted within an organization
through a mixture of formal and informal communications.
Although formal communication methods tend to take a
longer time to reach people than informal ones, they generally require less energy and result in less confusion and
fewer distortions. Formal communication methods usually
consist of memos, presentations, and scheduled meetings.
Within most of the best-run companies, there are three
types of regularly scheduled meetings to keep employees
informed: the weekly meeting, the quarterly meeting, and
the annual meeting.

The weekly meeting is used at all levels of a company to
help personnel stay abreast of particulars of the company's
operations.

At Delta Air Lines, the president meets with his team of
senior managers every Monday morning in order to discuss
the company's current problems, issues, and finances. After-

wards, the senior managers take their department heads to lunch to inform them about the substance of that morning's meeting. Then, upon returning from lunch, the department heads hold meetings with their immediate people and so on throughout the organization.

A similar series of meetings is held at Hewlett-Packard. H-P general managers hold meetings with their managers every Monday morning; these managers in turn meet with their team leaders during Monday afternoon; and they in turn have meetings with their team members by Tuesday afternoon. In this way all people in the company are routinely informed of important information about the business within forty-eight hours of the meeting of the general managers.

The second type of regularly scheduled meeting held by the best-run companies is a quarterly meeting (or a meeting held at some other regular interval over the course of the year). At this meeting, employees are brought up to date on the company's growth and activities so far that year. These meetings are also intended to nurture a family feeling among the people in the company.

Rene McPherson of Dana Corporation feels that if employees are involved in a communication process that gives them insight into the activities of the company, they will see themselves as a real part of the organization. Therefore he insists that all of their people get together at least quarterly to receive information on the company's performance as well as on any new developments. McPherson's theory is apparently working because the company's productivity record is improving yearly. When people are kept informed as to the results of their efforts, even if their results are below target, they are more inclined to improve performance than if they are not kept informed.

Physio-Control Corporation conducts quarterly meetings at which company employees are updated on what is going on in the business; they may be told of increases (or decreases) in sales from the last quarter, plans for the introduction of new products, or new goals for the future. Usually at these meetings the information is accompanied by a great deal of hoopla in order to generate enthusiasm and company spirit.

At Marion Laboratories, company chairman Ewing M. Kauffman uses his quarterly "Marion on the Move" meetings to inspire employees by updating them on the outcome of their efforts. All company people are in attendance at these meetings. The summer meeting is further highlighted by the awarding of bonus checks, profit sharing and incentive awards, and awards for employee suggestions.

The third type of regularly scheduled meeting is an annual meeting at which top management meets with company employees to inform them as to the overall progress of the company and to address their concerns and needs.

This annual meeting can take different forms. At Delta Air Lines, top-level management meets with all company people at least once a year in an open meeting where informative interchanges take place between managers and their people. In addition, management meets for four full days each year with flight attendants based in Atlanta. (Wouldn't it be wonderful if superintendents and their staffs spent four full days a year just talking to teachers?)

Whatever form the annual meeting takes, it is clear that the best-run companies will go to great lengths to have one.

Sam Johnson, chairman of S. C. Johnson & Son, actually chartered a 747 and flew 500 employees of its British subsidiary to the United States for one week of touring factories and sightseeing. When McPherson of Dana Corporation found out there was no facility large enough to hold all of his employees, he instructed management to clean out the shipping department and use it for a company meeting. And Hewlett-Packard and People Express have no reservations about bringing their people together from all parts of the country.

One of the finest communication systems I have come across has been implemented by Motorola. All of its people are organized into teams, and each team has one of its members on a steering committee at the next highest level in the organization. This committee, in turn, has a member on a committee at the next higher level. The steering committees have several roles:

- Coordination. Steering committees coordinate application of proposals that require cooperation among two or more teams.

- Lateral Communication. Steering committees disseminate the ideas, proposals, or practices of one team to other teams, thereby keeping everyone informed.

- Downward Communication. Steering committees ensure that each team has all of the managerial information necessary to perform its job.

- Upward Communication. Because each steering committee is linked to the next-higher-level steering committee, all problems, issues, and ideas eventually reach the company's top-level managers.

- Control. Steering committees negotiate objectives and performance standards with the teams that report to them.

- Evaluation. Based on the objectives and performance standards that have been decided upon with each team, steering committees assess the performance of the teams reporting to them and allocate rewards based on a predetermined formula.

In addition to this elaborate communication system, Motorola has adopted an "I Recommend" program. Every work area in the organization has a bulletin board on which people can post either signed or anonymous questions or recommendations, and supervisors are required to post a reply within seventy-two hours. If it is not possible for the supervisor to meet this deadline, he or she must post the name of the person who has been assigned to obtain the information and indicate a date by which a response will be posted.

Informal Communications

Although communication methods are vital to transmitting information within an organization, informal communications tend to be more effective in stimulating desired responses and generating ideas. One way that organizations can develop effective informal communications is by encouraging open communication through a policy or understanding that communications can and should cut across hierarchical lines. Almost all of the best-run companies are strong supporters of open communication. Rene McPherson of Dana Corporation requires that a minimum number of face-to-face meetings be conducted between division managers and everybody in the division so that they can discuss directly and specifically all matters pertaining to division results. McPherson also encourages face-to-face communication in in-house publications through features such as "Talk Back to the Boss" and "Ask Dumb Questions." Unlike many of the CEOs of not-so-excellent companies, McPherson feels that 40 to 50 percent of his time should be devoted to conferring directly with the people in the company. He conducts what he refers to as "town meetings" with all employees. Open communication is so important to Dana Corporation that it has been incorporated into a policy statement: "It is the job of all managers to keep Dana people informed. We believe direct communication with all of our people eliminates the need for a third party involvement. All managers shall periodically inform their people about the performance and plans of the operation."

Some companies support open communication through the physical arrangement of offices. Trammell Crow of Trammell Crow Company is one CEO who does not have a private office. He shares a large open space with other employees. Action stations or open space offices are becoming more common in the best-run companies because they allow people to talk to each other more freely.

There are basically three steps to promoting open communication:

Step one consists of adopting an open door policy. An open door policy states that any person on any level within an organization can have access, without going through the traditional chain of command, to anyone else including top management in order to make suggestions, to criticize, to offer ideas, to complain, to compliment, and even to cry a little.

Hewlett-Packard feels so strongly about its open door policy that it has stated explicitly what it expects from both management and their people:

- Managers/supervisors are expected to foster a work environment in which people feel free and comfortable to seek individual counsel and express general concerns.

- People have the right to discuss their concerns with higher-level managers. Any effort to intimidate or otherwise prevent an individual from going "up the line" is absolutely contrary to company policy and will be dealt with accordingly.

- An employee's use of the open door policy must not in any way influence evaluations of that employee or produce any other adverse consequences for the employee.

- People have open door responsibilities, too. They should keep their discussions with upper-level managers to the point and focused on concerns of significance.

Wang Labs has an open door policy which states that all meetings are open and that any employee can attend any company meeting. Delta Air Lines' open door policy stresses open and flowing communication, both vertically and horizontally, at all levels within the company. Delta's intent is to keep all employees aware of plans and significant events, whether they are favorable or unfavorable. Delta's management spends a great deal of time talking to company employees.

Step two in promoting open communications involves the implementation of visible management. Visible management is the practice by which managerial personnel go to employees to listen, to inform, and to facilitate understanding. The varied practices of the best-run companies reveal that there are essentially three techniques of visible management: management by wandering around, management by walking around, and management by socializing.

The technique of management by wandering around originated at Hewlett-Packard. It entails a dedication by top management to have frequent informal sessions with employees at all levels in the company. These sessions are supplemented by regular informal meetings such as extended coffee breaks at least once a month.

During the spring of each year, the president of Electro Scientific Industries conducts his own version of management by wandering around, called "Going well/I'm in the way" meeting, by gathering a group of twelve to fifteen people in a room and asking each of them individually what they find good and bad about the company. Although many of Electro's people initially were reluctant to fully open up, this is no longer the case: the people who attend these meetings are honest and frank with their comments. In addition to holding these meetings, the president meets once every three quarters with company divisions to announce Electro's pre-tax profits and other information.

Several CEOs of the best-run companies deserve awards for being devoted "wanderers." William Marriott, Jr. of Marriott Hotels travels 200,000 miles a year visiting installations in order to meet with company people. Ed Carlson, who took over the failing United Air Lines in 1970, traveled 200,000 miles that year touring company facilities across the United States and speaking to thousands of employees, informing them of changes in the operations of the airlines, listening to their concerns, and encouraging them to work harder at their own jobs. He also insisted that his top fifteen people do the same. And Sam Walton, who is the owner of WAL-MART Stores and is well over sixty-five years of age, travels more than 250,000 miles yearly, visiting each one of his more than 750 stores at least once.

What perplexes me is that somehow these people, who are the CEOs of multi-billion-dollar businesses, can find time to travel a quarter of a million miles a year to confer with hundreds of thousands of their employees while many of the superintendents of our larger school districts apparently do not have the time to travel twenty to fifty miles within their own school districts to meet with school people. It is high time for boards of education to demand that our chief school executives become "people" managers rather than "paper shufflers."

The second visible-management technique, management by walking around, is also known as the one-minute management approach. Essentially for plant managers and department supervisors, management by walking around requires that managerial personnel visit each one of their people each day for a brief period of time, i.e., plus or minus a minute, to confer with them, give them feedback, and provide explanations and assistance if needed. I make a distinction between management by wandering around and management by walking around by reserving the former for those located in the central office and the latter for those located in a building, department, or unit. However, central administrators and supervisors are also expected to practice management by walking around within their individual unit.

Hewlett-Packard declares what it desires from its managers in terms of management by walking around by stating, "To have a well-managed operation it is essential that the managers/supervisors be aware of what is happening in their areas—not just at their immediate level, but also at several levels below that." The company goes on to say, "Our people are our most important resource and the managers have direct responsibility for their training, their performance, and their general well-being. To do this, managers must get around to find out how their people feel about their jobs and what they feel will make their work more productive and more meaningful."

The third visible-management technique, management by socializing, requires that management meet informally with their people, usually over drinks and other refreshments, to discuss a host of business- and non-business-related matters. These meetings can be held either on or off company time. Tandem Computer makes use of beer parties and other recreational and social events to help employees become acquainted and thus facilitate on-the-job contact.

Knight-Ridder Newspapers has instituted what is know as "Management Coffee Breaks" whereby each newspaper's publisher regularly meets for 90 minutes with groups of 20 to 25 of its people to listen to and address their concerns as well as to facilitate understanding of the company's operations. Liebent Corporation is known for its once-a-month "Associates Luncheons" where, over a lunch costing one dollar and free drinks, employees get an opportunity to socialize in a non-business atmosphere. And Hewlett-Packard has what it refers to as "Communication Luncheons" at which top-level managers meet with groups of company people, fifteen or twenty at the most, with no supervisors present. Other company people know in advance who will be attending, and very often they pass on their own questions or complaints.

The format is usually the same. After light conversation to break down the barriers, someone will ask a question about something in the company that he or she does not understand or is unhappy about. This provides an opportunity to discuss company policy or company problems. Sometimes the items are trivial; sometimes the problems are strictly personal, and the manager must treat them with great care so as not to interfere with the supervisory process. Sometimes there is a pattern of problems (for example, inadequate supervisory training), which must be dealt with on a broad companywide basis. In any event, its people always learn more about how the company actually operates and, equally important, have a chance to hear first-hand what management is trying to do.

I believe it is appropriate at this point to identify one school person who has developed her own unique management-by-socializing method. Gladys Calhoun, principal of Jackson Academy of the East Orange School District in East Orange, New Jersey, is noted for her monthly communication breakfasts for teachers. At these delectable and free breakfasts, Ms. Calhoun addresses the concerns and issues of the group, discusses various operations and events in the school district, and encourages the teachers to share information on what is going on in their classrooms. Other school people have no doubt developed their own techniques, and they should be complimented for their creative communication efforts.

To encourage communication, the best-run companies also resort to a number of unusual and sometimes extreme ways of keeping their people informed.

Huiki Aldikati, chief of advanced vehicle design at Pontiac, hired a communicator, Tom Kalush. The role of the communicator was to do any communicating that Aldikati did not do and should have done. If Aldikati usurped the process to get to a given end, the communicator would either do what Aldikati should have done or cover for him. If Aldikati did not want to go to an important meeting, the communicator would go for him. Upon Kalush's return from the meeting, both parties would discuss the substance of the meeting and followup with appropriate action.

Eastern Air Lines had a communications committee that wanted to find out why People Express had replaced them as New York's No. 1 airline. So the committee elected two people to go to Newark and take a People Express plane. The two individuals observed, asked questions of stewardesses and passengers, listened, and took notes, all in an attempt to analyze the company's commitment to excellence.

Open communication is not restricted to oral communication. Tom Peters and Nancy Austin coined the phrase "all people are business people," which denotes a policy, often unwritten, that every person within a company is a full-scale member of the team and thus is entitled to almost any document of the organization. As a part of its open door policy, James C. Trebig of Tandem makes certain everyone has a copy of the strategic plan, including secretaries.

One case I think is interesting is that of the Dana Corporation, which during the 1981-1983 recession, had to lay off thousands of employees. Once a week during that period management sent an extensive newsletter to each of the laid-off employees as well as to those who were not laid off. This newsletter indicated the divisions and units affected by the layoff and others that might be affected. Dana prides itself on being a company that has instilled in its employees trust and tries hard to live up to that image even if it may hurt at times.

There are many other examples from the best-run companies of unique ways to maximize communication with employees. John W. Hanley, CEO of Monsanto, established a "green line" with a distinctive light on the telephone consoles of his top forty managers to improve the communication flow. Ian K. MacGregor of AMAX has been known to contact people in the company spontaneously and ask them, "What's new?" as a way to stay in touch with the communication flow. And several years ago Hewlett-Packard retained the services of the International Survey Corporation in order to:

- give people a chance to express opinions about their work place;

- provide the company with an opportunity to hear the concerns of its people;

- compare the company with other large companies in terms of the attitudes of employees; and

- set a standard or benchmark for future surveys.

Significantly, this survey was not a one-way program; the survey results were made known to H-P employees. Where there appeared to be deficiencies, positive remedial actions were taken and these too were reported.

Recommendations for School Districts

On the basis of the experiences of the best-run companies, I make the following recommendations to help school districts improve their formal communications:

- A school district's central administration team should hold weekly meetings to discuss programs, progress toward goals and objectives, budgetary matters, and other districtwide activities. It is recommended that these meetings be held on Monday mornings and that they last no more than two hours. After these meetings the central administrators should arrange to meet with their principals during the afternoon session on Monday. Then all principals should meet with their school people during the after school session on Tuesday. Obviously, the agenda for all the principals' meetings should be similar. School districts should hold quarterly progress report meetings to update school people as to various performance indicators of the school district, such as academic achievement results, SAT scores, awards received, attendance rates, etc. A monthly meeting of the schools and other departments and units should be held to inform school people of requirements, needs, and expectations, as well as district and unit matters.

- School districts should hold two different types of annual meetings. An annual orientation meeting should be held in August or September to bring all school people up to date on matters relating to the opening day of school. This meeting should also include an inspirational presentation to fan enthusiasm about where the school district is heading. Then in May or June there should be an annual state of the school district meeting to inform all school and community people about the performance of the school district that year and aspirations for the ensuing year. During this meeting school people should be congratulated for their efforts and outstanding contributions should be recognized. All school people should be invited to attend these meetings. The fact is that no one person or group of individuals is less important than any other in a school district's efforts to achieve excellence. When secretaries, teachers' aides, custodians, and other school people are invited to attend the annual meetings, both their feeling of belonging to the school "family" and their self-esteem are enhanced.

Some superintendents will most likely say that they have too many people to call all of them together in one setting to conduct annual meetings. There are two ways to lick this problem. One is to arrange for all people to convene in an available facility in the community. Sometimes an owner of a local theatre is willing to let the theater be used for this purpose either for free or for a nominal charge. The other is to arrange for all people from certain groups of schools to meet in a common area. However, if this is done schools should not be segregated according to level (elementary, middle, secondary).

Again drawing from the practices and policies of the best-run companies, I make the following recommendations to help schools improve their informal communications.

- The superintendent, central administrators, and supervisors should practice management by wandering around, by talking with people in all schools, departments, and units. This activity should take up a minimum of 25 percent of the central administrator's time. In addition, these school administrators should practice management by walking around by conferring with the people in their own offices.

- Principals and other buildingwide directors and supervisors should practice management by walking around, or the one-minute management approach, by meeting daily with every building or unit school person for a minute or so to talk, listen, and facilitate understanding regarding school or unit matters as well as personal concerns.

- All school administrators should attend a minimum of 90 percent of the social affairs attended by school people in order to practice management by socializing.

- The superintendent, central administrators, and supervisors should have coffee or lunch with groups of school people at least once a month to listen to their concerns and to solicit from them information on what they like most and least about the school district.

- Teachers should practice management of the instructional process by walking around the classroom and meeting personally with every student for one minute or more every day.

Strategies for Achieving Excellence

- Conduct an informal assessment of the communications of your school district by randomly asking a number of school people, such as, teachers, secretaries, and others—the following questions:

  –Who are the top-level school administrators of the school district?
  –What is the most recent program implemented in the school district?
  –How much does the school district spend educating each student?
  –What are the long-range goals of the school district?
  –What are the names of all of the members of the board of education?

  Devise your own rating scale for evaluating the results of this informal communications assessment of your school district. Prepare and implement a plan for improving the communication processes of the school district.

- Every year give annual plaques to the central administrator, director, and supervisor who are the "best wanderers."

- Insist that principals as well as unit and department leaders know all of their people by first and last names.

- Conduct meetings in other people's offices.

- Let people know that the district's central administrators make a practice of managing by wandering around.

- Schedule a specific time each day to manage by wandering around, say from 11:00 to 2:00.

- Periodically visit the offices of principals and inquire as to whether or not they have completed their one-minute management practices.

- Do what Thomas Anderson, President of H. B. Fuller Company, does. He makes himself available to everyone in the company through what is referred to as "the President's Hot Line." By using this special toll-free number, anybody in the company can contact him to complain about or to praise a supervisor, to present ideas and suggestions for improving a service or product, or to discuss anything on his or her mind.

- Emulate Pitney Bowes by distributing not only an annual report to stockholders but one to job holders. That company also holds annual job holders' meetings with groups of about 250 to 300 company people. At these meetings, which usually last two to three hours, employees can ask management questions about anything related to the company. Those people who have the best oral and written questions receive a $25 savings bond. Similar meetings could be conducted in schools, with the principal orchestrating the meeting and a central administrator responding to queries. The superintendent should attend as many of these meetings as possible. The school district could either finance the best-question awards or request that local business do so.

- Develop a formal communication assessment instrument similar to the one described on pages

75-79 in the book *Leadership—Strategies for Organizational Effectiveness* by James J. Cribbin. Use this assessment instrument to determine communication groups at individual schools and develop an action plan for closing the gaps. Then retain a communication expert and have him or her evaluate your assessment and action plan. After making any necessary changes, discuss the assessment and plan of action with school people, and then put the plan into effect.

Reach Decisions
by Consensus

Consensus . . . can be a powerful tool for building . . .
unity and strength and for choosing wise, creative
courses of action.

—MILTON AVERY

What is consensus and why should it be used in our
schools?

Consensus decision making is a process by which a team
or group cooperatively arrives at a mutually acceptable decision that all members agree to support. It is the most effective way to get a maximum number of people involved in the
decision-making process as well as to get their commitment
to the decision arrived at by the team. Someone once said
that 100 organized men committed to a common objective
would conquer 1,000. And John Hancock is reported to have
said that he preferred to react to a decision that was only 50
percent technically correct but embraced by a group with 90
percent enthusiasm over one that was 90 percent technically
correct but embraced with only 50 percent enthusiasm.
Although consensus decision making is the best way yet
developed to arrive at decisions that will generate such a
high level of satisfaction or commitment, few of our school
districts use this process to make decisions. This must
change if we are to achieve excellence in education.

Let's compare two decision-making processes, both
involving the purchase of word processors. The first took

place on Long Island, New York. The superintendent of schools decided to buy word processors for five departments of the central administrative office, so he charged one of his assistants with the responsibility of researching the subject and presenting him with several choices. He made a selection from that list, called in the representative for a demonstration, and then had his secretary try out the equipment. When he was satisfied that his secretary had no negative comments about the machine, he ordered five processors for over $20,000.

A different decision-making process was used at Hoffman-LaRoche. Since secretaries were going to be the primary users of the word processing equipment, management felt that they were best qualified to make a selection among the various kinds of available word processing hardware and software. After visiting IBM, Xerox, Exxon, and other producers of word processors, the secretaries reached a consensus on the one word processor that would best meet all of their needs.

Several months after the school district received its word processors, I visited a few of the departments and queried the secretaries about their word processors. Although most of them had no complaints, none appeared to be entirely committed to the equipment either. In fact, it turned out that the word processors were only being used from 10 percent to 30 percent of the time. Incidentally, the manufacturer of the word processor stopped producing them, and as a result the school district may experience some difficulty in getting someone to service its equipment. On the other hand, the secretaries at Hoffman-LaRoche are reported to be extremely happy with their word processors and the equipment is being used most of the day.

Why did the school superintendent use an authoritarian rather than a consensus approach to decision making? Well, there are many possible explanations. Far too many school districts are in a rush to make decisions and therefore often do so at the expense of the people who will be most affected by the decision. Far too many school administrators are bent on being dictatorial, even though countless studies have indicated that more can be accomplished with people when they are involved in the decision-making process. Far too many school administrators are not willing to share their power with school people, completely ignoring the fact that many heads are usually better than one. Far too many school administrators have reached the stage of obsolescence and are fixed on outmoded ways in their treatment of school people. Finally, far too many administrators have not been properly trained in the various techniques that give their people opportunities to become meaningfully involved in solving problems and making decisions.

Consensus Decision Making in Business

The technique of consensus management was developed in this country during the 1940s and 1950s, but it was eventually abandoned by most companies because of the time it involved.

However, the Japanese saw value in the concept and gave it new life during the 1960s and 1970s. In *Theory Z*, William Ouchi describes how the Japanese use consensus: "When an important decision needs to be made . . . everyone who will feel its impact is involved in making it. In the case of a decision on where to put a new plant, whether to change a production process or some other major event, that will often mean sixty to eighty people directly involved in making the decision. A team of three will be assigned the duty of talking to all sixty to eighty people and, each time a significant modification arises, contacting all the people involved again. The team will repeat this process until a true consensus has been achieved."

The success of Japanese companies during the 1970s led American business and industry to explore Japanese management techniques and practices, many of which had originated in the United States. One such technique was management by consensus, and today a number of America's best-run companies use consensus. A large developer of office buildings, industrial parks, and warehouses, Trammel Crow, is owned by eighty regional partners who use a consensus style of management to determine what projects to build and how to build them. Kollmorgen Corporation makes sophisticated electro-optical instruments, electrical motors and controls, and printed circuit boards. It is organized around several autonomous divisions, each with its own president and a board of directors composed of divisional peers and other top managers. Each board is required to arrive at decisions using consensus. Majority vote is not permissible. At Procter & Gamble, the judgment of a single manager, including the CEO, counts no more or less than that of another employee. This company pays its managers not for making judgments but for removing judgment. Procter & Gamble has a long-standing tradition of operating through committees that use consensus in making major decisions.

Advantages and Disadvantages of Consensus

Using the consensus decision-making process has many advantages or benefits. Research evidence indicates that the process generates decisions that are more creative than those arrived at by individuals. Consensus decisions reflect the synthesis and integration of many ideas rather than the selection of just one.

People are more committed to decisions reached by consensus because they have had a part in making them and understand the rationale behind them; the process works through gradual persuasion rather than coercion. In addition, decisions made by consensus tend to be implemented more quickly and with little change.

The consensus process helps improve employee self-esteem because everyone gets to contribute. The participants get the feeling that others appreciate their ideas and concerns.

Finally, the process promotes a team spirit in several ways. For one, it helps the team function as a group rather than an aggregate of individuals. Second, it requires honesty, open communications, and a free exchange of ideas. Third, unlike majority rule, which inevitably results in a loss for an individual or a side, consensus decision making fosters a win-win mentality. And fourth, it nurtures an understanding that the integrity of the team is more important than any single issue.

One major disadvantage of the consensus decision-making process is the time and patience required to arrive at a decision. Although sometimes consensus can take less time than voting, at other times it may take as much as a year to reach a decision that is acceptable to all members of the team. Also, consensus decision making requires more training, more thought, and more energy than individual decision making. However, when all of its pluses and minuses are added up, one conclusion stands out: school administrators have more to gain than to lose by implementing the process in our schools.

Suggested Uses of Consensus in Schools

The time is ripe for school administrators to explore the use of the consensus decision-making process. I believe it can be profitably used by schools to make a number of decisions, including:

- Decision concerning the hiring of teachers. Prospective teachers could be screened and interviewed by a team composed of staff from the human resources office and teachers from the appropriate grade or department. This team would use consensus to make a selection or selections which would then be approved (or rejected) by the principal.

- Decisions about student rules and regulations. The team in this case could be composed of students, teachers, administrators, and parents.

- All departmental building decisions. (Although a policy mandating the use of consensus in making these decisions might generate a great deal of resentment from principals, this should diminish with time and experience.)

- Many of the decisions issued by the superintendent's office. These decisions could be made by the superintendent and his or her cabinet using consensus.

- Decisions about a school's budget (provided the superintendent has already established a firm budget figure). The team making the budget decisions could be composed of parents, teachers, administrators, and students.

In addition, consensus could be used by a group of school and community people in developing the school district's statement of philosophy.

A Description of the Consensus Process

Implementing the consensus decision-making process is relatively easy and requires only a few basic steps.

The first step is to prepare either a proposal setting out what the team must do to fulfill its charge or an agenda specifying the items to be considered, the action required, and the presenter. The agenda can be established either prior to the discussion or during the meeting. The advantage of establishing the agenda during the meeting is that everyone has a say about what should be discussed and in what sequence.

The team leader introduces the proposal or agenda item to the team, defines the problem, provides as much background information as possible and recommends an approach to the problem. Particularly when an impromptu meeting has been called to find a solution to a problem, the introduction should contain a precise definition of the proposal or item to be discussed and a clear statement of what has to be done to arrive at a consensus. This statement should focus on either what has to be accomplished or what problem must be solved by the decision. If the goal is already stated in the proposal, discussion should be focused on identifying performance standards that need to be achieved to reach the goal. If the goal as well as the performance standards must be mutually agreed upon by the team members, discussion should focus on determining the primary purpose of the meeting and how it should be realized.

Team members then respond to the proposal or item, offering their own ideas and opinions. Their comments may or may not be influenced by the ideas and opinions already offered by other team members.

As long as the ideas and opinions presented are relevant to the original proposal or item, the team leader encourages the team members to continue. The team leader should try to keep the discussion moving along in an orderly and productive fashion by:

- keeping members from meandering

- probing for more ideas and opinions

- providing clarity by rephrasing unclear or complicated statements

- pointing out where agreements and disagreements exist

- citing new issues and problems when they arise

- making certain that all viewpoints, reservations, impressions, feelings, and concerns are heard and understood by the total team membership

- noting process problems and working them through.

When most viewpoints have been stated and team members begin to repeat themselves, the team leader asks if anything new can be added to the discussion. If there are no further comments, he or she tests for a consensus by stating the position (solution) toward which the team seems to have been moving.

The team then reacts to the "consensus" test of the team leader. The team leader makes certain that all concerns and objections are voiced by going from one team member to another, noting both verbal and nonverbal responses.

Team members listen to each concern and discussion ensues. When it again seems as though a consensus has been reached, the team leader states the new position that the team appears to have arrived at. If there are no more objections, all team members sign the position statement. Responsibilities for carrying out the decision are then assigned to team members.

At times, for example, when there is a time constraint, the decision that is arrived at may not entirely satisfy every team member, but they may be willing to accept it as the best decision that could be agreed to at that time under those circumstances. Under no circumstances should the team be coerced or pressured into accepting a decision. Such action would effectively negate vital by-products of consensus, such as team member commitment to the decision and improved coordination.

If consensus cannot be reached, a situation that usually means that team members do not have enough information to render a good decision, the decision will have to be deferred until the team members can be given more information and more discussion can take place.

Some Guidelines

I have found the following guidelines to be helpful in facilitating the consensus decision-making process:

- Consensus meetings should be conducted as if they were friendly gatherings of friends rather than tense contests between opposing sides. Robert's Rules of Order and consensus tend to be incompatible.

- Team members must resist blindly arguing for their points of view, which often leads to confrontation. Instead, they must present their position in a clear and logical manner and listen actively to other positions, carefully considering what others have to offer.

- Team members should refrain from changing their minds merely to avoid an argument or conflict. They should agree to a decision only when they are convinced that the reasons for it make good sense and are logical.

- The attitude among team members should be "I win—you win." When a true consensus has been reached, everybody has a share of the pie.

- All team members must participate in the discussion, and they should encourage other members to participate.

- Each team member should summarize the statement of the previous speaker before presenting his or her own point of view.

- From time to time the team leader should review the course of the discussion in order to clarify ideas and to point out similarities and differences in points of view.

- When team members become emotional or tense or when nothing is being said, the team leader should call for a brief recess.

- If a tentative decision is reached, the consensus should be tested by bringing in an expert to discuss the decision or by leaving the final decision to a follow-up meeting.

- If a final decision is reached, the team leader should review with the team what each member has agreed to do to implement the solution.

- Remember: Consensus does not mean that everyone must be equally satisfied with the decision reached. However, everyone must be comfortable with the decision and should feel that it is the best that could be arrived at given the time and circumstances. If anyone continues to have serious reservations, he or she has the right to "block" the decision, and the team must either continue to discuss it until the team member finds it acceptable or arrive at a new decision.

Variations on Consensus

Sometimes arriving at a consensus may not be possible or may not be worth the time and effort required. In those cases, there are two alternatives that can be used.

The first alternative involves consensus with an exception. The team leader presents a proposal to the team, and individual members indicate whether they favor the proposal, can live with it, or are uncomfortable with it. If no one is uncomfortable with the proposal, the decision is implemented. If some members are uncomfortable with it, they are requested to state their reasons and a discussion ensues. After the discussion, the team leader asks the team if the idea should be implemented over the objections of the minority. A negative vote means postponing the decision until a consensus can be reached through discussion.

The second alternative involves consensus by committee. If there is a major objection to the proposed solution, the team breaks up into mini-teams to discuss the problem and to develop new proposals, amendments, etc. The larger team then reconvenes to see if a consensus can be reached. If there are still team members who object to the proposal, they are asked to step aside and let the majority rule on the solution. If those objecting to the proposal refuse to step aside, a committee is formed which represents the various opinions expressed. After this committee has met and reached a mutually acceptable proposal, the proposal is brought back to the team for final decision. If a consensus is still not realized, the team will vote to accept the decision of a majority, which is usually three-fourths of the membership. A vote is then conducted, and the proposal is accepted if it receives the approval of the majority.

Strategies for Achieving Excellence

- Acquire a number of copies of *Building United Judgment* (published by the Center for Conflict Resolution, 731 State Street, Madison, WI 53703) and use it to train school people in implementing consensus decision making.

- Publish in the school newsletter articles about situations in which consensus has been reached and the impact of those decisions.

- Prepare a policy statement that specifies those situations in which it is appropriate to use consensus decision making and/or one of the alternatives.

- Contact the companies that have been identified in this lesson as using consensus and see if a few school people can sit in on one of their decision-making sessions.

- Prepare a paper on how to arrive at consensus and circulate it throughout the school district.

- Organize a one-day workshop on consensus decision making for all school people.

- Retain a training consulting firm to create a training film on how to implement consensus decision making.

- Use a trained facilitator the first three or four times the consensus process is used.

• LESSON 6 •

Become Close to Kids

This could be a time for schools and youth to come to
know one another, an opportunity for them to behave
"with" rather than "at" each other.
— SAMUEL A. MOORE II

Although a customer is to a company what a student is
to a school district, the two are certainly not treated in the
same way. The best-run companies are close to their customers. In Tom Peters's words, "The best-run companies
smell like their customers, . . . the customers permeate
every fiber of these companies." He goes on to say that these
companies cherish their salespersons because they are the
ones closest to the customers. In public education, very few
school districts think of their kids as customers, very few of
them "smell" of their students, and few of them cherish
their teachers.

The Best Value Their Customers

To the best-run companies, the customer is everything.
This is made very clear, for example, in one of Hewlett-
Packard's corporate objectives: "[We intend] to provide products and services of the highest quality and the greatest
possible value to our customers, thereby gaining and holding their respect and loyalty." The company explains: "The
continued growth and success of our company will be
assured only if we offer our customers innovative products
that fill real needs and provide lasting value, and that are

76

supported by a wide variety of useful services, both before and after sale. Satisfying customer needs requires the active participation of everyone in the company. It demands a total commitment to quality, a commitment that begins in the laboratory and extends into every phase of our operations. Careful attention to quality not only enables us to meet or exceed customer expectations, but it also has a direct and substantial effect on our operations costs and profitability. Good communications are essential to an effective field sales effort. Because of our broad and growing line of products, very often several sales teams will be working with a single customer. These teams must work closely to assure that the products recommended best fulfill the customer's overall, long-term needs. Moreover, HP customers must feel that they are dealing with one company, a company with common policies and services, and one that has a clear understanding of their needs and a genuine interest in providing proper, effective solutions to their problems."

One of the pillars underlying the growth of Advanced Micro Devices is the company's commitment to its customers. At AMD, the customer is king and queen. The company maintains that ". . . we depend on them for continued growth, and they depend on us for continued product innovation, product quality and service. We at AMD take care to maintain this relationship; from product definition and design to wafer fabrication to marketing, we give our best to see that the customer gets the best." Celestial Seasonings also believes that its customers are kings and queens and spells out its commitment to them. It maintains that its past, current, and future successes are a result of a total dedication to excellent customer service. The company says, "Satisfying our customer and consumer needs in a superior way is the only reason we are in business, and we shall proceed with an obsession to give wholeheartedly to those who buy our products."

Techniques Used by the Best Companies

What are the best-run companies doing to build those relationships with customers? Hewlett-Packard's personal computer division operates focus groups in which company managers meet with potential customers. These groups help the company come up with products that meet the interests and needs of customers. To improve its customer relations, Air Freight Corporation embarked on a behavior modification program. The goal of the company was to respond to customers' concerns within a 90-minute time frame. However, research had indicated that this goal was being achieved only 30 percent of the time. Therefore, in an effort to improve their people's response to customers, the company's representatives were requested to keep log sheets on which they indicated the actual time it took to answer each customer's query. These sheets were then checked daily by management, and immediate feedback was given to the representatives as to their performance. Whenever the representatives improved their response rate to customers, they were rewarded with praise from supervisors. In fact, efforts were recognized and praised even when performance standards were not met; representatives not meeting the standards were praised for their honesty in maintaining accurate records and reminded about the need to meet the 90-minute goal.

Procter & Gamble's commitment to customers, referred to as "mania consumerism," has taken a variety of forms—from testing products in kitchens to hiring housewives to provide feedback on new products, sending large quantities of free samples, and conducting over 1.5 million telephone interviews annually. The company is especially known for actively listening to its customers. It was the first company to put the number of its toll-free 800 telephone line on all of its packaging; this line, the company maintains, is a major source of product ideas. In 1979 alone the company received 200,000 calls from customers who had complaints or ideas for new and existing products. According to Tom Peters and Bob Waterman, all of the best-run companies are not only better on service, quality, and reliability but also better about listening to customers. As a result, the customer is truly in a partnership with these companies.

How Schools Can Become Close to Kids

What can school districts learn from the best-run companies in terms of becoming close to students? Before I answer that question, I should explain what I mean by being close. Several signs are evident when a school district is really close to its kids:

- The district uses an assortment of ways to determine the needs and desires of its kids and actively tries to meet those needs.

- Kids are given opportunities to help solve problems related to their schools.

- Building administrators religiously practice management by walking around, by talking and listening to kids.

- Teachers in the classroom practice management by walking around, by "connecting" with each kid for least one minute every day.

- Kids have several avenues to reach school people in the event of need or problems.

- An assessment is conducted periodically to determine the extent to which the school is relating to needs of kids, and plans are then developed and executed in accordance with the assessment's findings.

There are a number of ways in which a school district can become close to kids. A relatively new but essential way involves the development of a strategic curriculum. Ideally the job of a project team consisting of students, parents, and school people, development of such a curriculum is based on a determination of the future needs of students over a ten-year period. To identify these needs the project team might attend seminars on future trends, read and discuss appropriate books and articles, visit other school districts that have also undertaken this effort, and even invite futurists to discuss their thoughts on future trends that will affect education and the life of students. The information gathered in these ways should then be used by the team to identify the strengths, weaknesses, and gaps in the present curriculum in relation to the future needs of students, to determine the concepts and skills necessary to eliminate the weaknesses and the gaps. The project should be started in the high school and moved downward throughout other grades. Less student and more professional involvement will be necessary in the lower grades.

Another method for bringing a school district close to kids—one that has been used by some of the best school districts around the nation—is surveying and interviewing graduates to determine their ideas as to how the school district could have been more helpful to them. This survey should ask students the following questions:

- What academic subjects helped them the most? The least?

- What more can the school do to prepare students to meet the "outside world"?

- What can teachers do, stop doing, or do differently to help kids become better prepared for post–high school life?

- In what aspects of post–high school life have students found it difficult to function because of a lack of high school preparation?

- In what aspect(s) of post–high school life have kids found it easy to function because of their high school preparation?

- What new or additional courses should be added to the high school program? What courses should be eliminated?

- Which group of school professionals—i.e., math teachers, guidance counselors, etc.—helped kids the most?

When the surveys have been returned, the answers should be compiled and a preliminary report prepared. This report should be submitted to the respondents to see whether they agree or disagree with the essence of the report. The final report should be reviewed by the professional staff, and concrete steps should then be taken to accommodate the needs of students.

Quality circles are another tool that school districts can use to improve student relations. In industry, where they have been in use for several years, quality circles consist of teams of from three to eleven employees working in the same unit who meet for about one hour a week to resolve job-related problems. I believe the first student quality circle was established in Northern Regional Valley High School in northern New Jersey. To start the program, the superintendent, who was a certified facilitator, trained several high school students and two teachers in the problem-solving methods of quality circles. Students were excused from classes to attend the training sessions. After about ten hours of training, they then engaged in identifying, selecting, and solving problems within the high school. When a solution was approved by the high school administration, a student from the circle used the PA system to announce to the student body the original problem as well as its solution. What was the first problem/solution? The circle recommended that the height of the water fountains be raised so that it would be easier for students to take a drink (this problem had gone unnoticed by the high school administration for seven years). In addition to concrete solutions to specific problems, the superintendent reports that the following also resulted from the quality circle program:

- Students got to know the superintendent better, as well as the teachers involved.

- Because the circle members conducted a survey and interviewed students, they got a broad-based view of the school's problems as perceived by students.

- Other students became interested in the quality circle concept.

- Other teachers became curious about the project and indicated an interest in establishing teacher quality circles.

- Parents of the circle's student members respected the efforts of the school district to adopt a concept that was working in business and industry.

One of the most effective ways for school people to become close to kids is for them to become close to parents. Although most school districts use some traditional ways to become close to parents—parent/teacher conferences, Parent/ Teacher Association meetings, telephone conversations, and correspondence —I shall identify some other methods that could prove useful.

- Instead of the traditional parent/teacher conferences, I recommend that there be parent/teacher/ student conferences. After all, why shouldn't the person who is the subject of the conference be included?

- If parents don't come out to school-related meetings, why not conduct neighborhood school meetings to discuss school issues? These could be held on Sunday afternoons at the homes of key families identified by social workers. Students should be encouraged to attend these meetings.

- Parents of students who have perfect attendance records could receive congratulatory letters recognizing them for the part they played in getting their children to school.

- The traditional report card could be revised to include a section in which parents are graded on attending school affairs, voting on the school budget, participating in school events, and helping their children with their homework.

- Aspects of school work could be taped so that parents could assist their children in their studies.

- Parent/student awards could replace some student awards, and additional awards could be given to the combinations of student, parent, and teacher who have done the most for the school.

- School superintendents and other school administrators could institute "knowing parents by wandering around," by visiting homes, communities, and local agencies and by "preaching and teaching" at church affairs.

Another way that school districts can become close to kids is by using a technique employed by Quad/Graphics. This company has instituted what is referred to as "management by walking away" in which all managers leave the plant for twenty-four hours, putting operations in the hands of their people. I believe that such a program could be successfully adopted by high schools as long as careful planning is conducted by joint teacher/student/administrator teams. During such a day, the president of the student council could be the high school principal, and other student council representatives could function as either school administrators or department heads. All classes could be taught by students who are high achievers in specific subject areas. In some states, there may be a law against holding classes without a certified teacher present. If this is the case in your area, the program can be modified to have teachers stationed in the classroom merely as observers. Not only could such a program bring the school closer to the students but it would provide experience that is much more rewarding than the traditional "senior class day."

Taking another cue from the best-run companies, I also propose that school districts establish an achievement review team consisting of parents, students, and school people. Outside of the board of education, this would be the most powerful group in the school district; it would be established and supported by the superintendent, whose office would back all of the team's efforts. The job of this team would be to determine why the district's programs are or are not producing academic achievement, what program improvements are needed, and what must be done to bring improvements to the school district. The needs of students would be the team's primary concern; politics and funds would be considered secondary. Among its activities, this team could visit other school districts to observe innovative programs and, if one looks interesting, request that a project team be appointed and given extra compensation or time to plan and develop a similar program for the district. This team could also undertake studies of specific problems—for example, why the SAT scores of district students are not improving—in which they look at various solutions, select one they consider best, and have this solution reviewed by an expert to determine if it is really viable. As yet another activity, the team could request that a principal from a school where achievement was poor meet with the team to explain why students are not achieving, to discuss what is being done to upgrade the education in that school, and to present a plan for achieving excellence. Can a review team be successful in effecting change? Yes, but only if the board of education and the superintendent have the guts to support its efforts.

One day when I was conducting a workshop for about fourteen superintendents and assistant superintendents I asked them, "How many of you have taken time out from your 'paper shuffling' schedule to visit your schools, to chit-chat with students, eat lunch with them and informally participate in classroom discussions?" Not to my surprise, the answer turned out to be none. That's unfortunate; the superintendent and central administrators should function as role models in becoming close to kids. I am reminded of an experience I had as a superintendent. It took place during the sensitivity movement in the latter part of the 1960s. The director of the local community college felt it would be a good idea for me to get to know the problem students in the high school and for them to get to know me, so he set a meeting date. At this meeting I was positioned in the center of the room, with the students seated all around me. First, the students had their chance to have their say about me, and they criticized me for sitting in a "white tower" and not getting to know them. They were very emotional. I displayed no emotion and waited for a chance to present myself to them. I knew that once I had conveyed to them my background and the poverty I had experienced—once I had my day in court—they would be able to relate to me. I turned out to be right. When I spoke about how I lived and grew up, I was no longer a stranger to these students but one of them. The meeting concluded with the students' shaking my hand and embracing me, and I subsequently gave them an opportunity to follow me around for an entire day to see how the school district was managed. During that day, the students attended meetings with me and my staff and observed while I made telephone calls, conferred with new employees, and participated in a number of other activities. At day's end, they went home with an improved perspective on both the school district and myself as well as enhanced self-esteem.

Superintendents and central administrators are not the only ones who are not close to kids; many high school principals are also strangers to their kids. On a visit to a high school on the west coast, I once asked a student the name of the high school principal and she gave me the name of the assistant principal. When I told her that person was not the principal but the assistant principal, she retorted, "Then I don't know who the principal is." On a visit to another high school, this one on the east coast, a parent I know saw a couple of students kissing and embracing in one of the school corridors. When she asked them if they couldn't find a better place to do this, they responded, "What better place is there than the high school?" Just then the male student exposed himself. This incident was related to the principal but nothing was done about it. One day I had an opportunity to visit this same high school and saw groups of students inside and outside the school smoking marijuana. When I told the superintendent and principal about what I had observed, the principal laughed at me and said, "What else is new?" The reason these incidents and others like them are occurring in countless high schools around the nation is the lack of "visible management" by many principals. I know of one high school in Massachusetts in which a troubled principal had barricaded himself from students and teachers by setting up a chain and closing two doors leading to his office—until I as superintendent insisted that he remove the chains and open the doors.

Al Vidal, principal of the George Washington High School in San Francisco, is one of those principals who have a passion for kids. Don't look for him in his office, because Vidal manages by wandering around. Look for him in the school corridors, in the cafeteria, in the classrooms, and out on the playing fields. He may be congratulating a student for winning a scholastic award or playing well on the basketball court; he may be questioning a student to see if she has done her homework; he may be inquiring about a member of a student's family who is ill; he may be joking with a group of students; he may be talking with a student about a serious personal problem the student is experiencing. Vidal will do everything and anything to help his kids because he cares for them. What's more, his passion is reciprocated; whenever he comes into the auditorium during a school meeting and goes up onto the stage, thunderous applause breaks out from the students. You see, the kids know and appreciate when someone cares about them.

To help school districts become close to kids, our high school accreditation agencies must also acquire some "guts" and insist that accrediting teams tell the "whole truth and nothing but the truth" when they visit and review high schools. In far too many instances, they hold back in their reports because they don't want to hurt the feelings of their colleagues. I maintain that a team's reports should be scrupulously honest even if it hurts, because the team's first allegiance should be to the kids.

When a high school is striving for excellence, it should be doing so on a continuous basis. I also recommend that all visitations by accrediting teams be unannounced because, unfortunately, what often happens when the date and time are announced for an accrediting team's visit is that the high school sets up a "facade"; then, after the team leaves, it's back to the normal routine, which is usually the not-so-excellent way of operating a high school.

Proper training of all staff is an important element in achieving closeness. School districts should emulate IBM, which backs up its close-to-the-customer objective with intensive training of its sales force. In reference to school districts, I envision that such training would be conducted at the district's training center, by inside and outside consultants. Both teachers and school administrators would be required to undergo a minimum number of hours of training in the following areas:

- establishing an intimate relationship with kids and parents

- relating to parents as equals

- the do's and don't of home visits

- connecting with difficult students

- how to demonstrate caring to kids and parents

- how to confer, listen, probe, and facilitate

- using the one-minute management approach in the classroom

School administrators and perhaps teachers would also receive additional training in areas such as management by walking around, improving memory, the art of listening, one-minute management techniques for recognizing and rewarding excellence, participating in community affairs, etc.

Student awards are a method that schools have used for years to become close to kids. In addition to awards already being given, include a few others that are team oriented—that is, instead of being given to individual students, the awards would be given to teams.

- Give awards to teams or classes of students who have improved attendance beyond a certain standard jointly agreed to by the school district and students.

- When students excel in two or three areas, such as attendance, academic progress, and participation in school affairs, give awards to the students, members of their families, and their teachers.

- Give awards to teams or classes of students who have done the most for the community.

- Give awards to teams or classes of students who have submitted suggestions having the greatest impact on the school district.

Strategies for Achieving Excellence

- Prepare a student-oriented proclamation and circulate it throughout the district. This proclamation should include statements similar to the following:

-When students experience a problem with services or resources, it is the school district's problem, not the students'.

-When students fail, it means that the school district has failed students.

-When students drop out of school, it means that the school district has failed to provide students with an appealing learning environment.

- Encourage elementary principals to do what M. H. Messinger of Berkeley, California does—he meets, in their homes, with the families of new students who are going to be admitted to his school. Messinger then shares any pertinent information about the child with his school people.

- Consider doing the following to help the school district become close to students.

    -Train teachers to detect students who have been abused. (Such a program already exists in numerous school districts around the nation, including the Great Neck School District on Long Island, New York).

    -Train teachers to detect potential suicide victims.

    -Establish a 24-hour hot line for students who are experiencing problems with drugs and alcohol.

- Maintain computerized profiles on all students so that teachers can get the information they need at a moment's notice. The profile should contain the student's record as well as listing his or her interests, skills, strengths, and weaknesses. Also included could be recommendations for meeting the specific socio-economic, physical, and emotional needs of the student.

90

- Take this student closeness test:

    –Does your school district have a program or some other means to listen to students?

    –Do your school administrators spend a minimum of 25 percent of their time walking around the school and playground area just talking and listening to kids?

    –Does your school district periodically conduct a survey to determine student needs, interests, expectations, and aspirations?

    –Has your school district organized a team composed of students and school people to critically review the curriculum every year in order to determine if it is meeting student needs, interests, expectations, and aspirations?

    –Can you cite several instances in which the school district broke routine to satisfy a special need, interest, expectation, or aspiration of kids?

    –Does your school district have a program in which new families who have moved into the school district are contacted by phone and welcomed?

- Publish a semi-monthly publication entitled "Close Encounters with Kids" to detail the efforts of school people to satisfy the needs, interests, expectations, and aspirations of students.

- Establish a procedure by which students, without identifying themselves, can make complaints about the schools.

- Invite students to meet with the superintendent without any other school people present and have them describe what they like most and least about their schools. Then take action to meet their criticisms, and report back to the students.

- Organize an "idea" team to interview students in order to solicit ideas about how the school district could become close to kids.

- Establish a student "hot line" manned by administrators on a weekly basis. Encourage students to use this hot line any time they have a problem or would like to discuss something.

- Prepare a Student Needs Assessment Survey and administer it to all students. Once the answers have been analyzed and ranked, report the findings to students, as well as the steps that will be taken to accommodate their needs.

- Periodically organize all-day meetings in which educational-product dealers meet both students and teachers to discuss educational products, programs, and services that may be useful to students.

- Make arrangements for a team of students to visit other schools noted for excellence in order to investigate services and programs that could be implemented in your school district.

- Emulate the Chicago school system by establishing a program not only to provide education relating to sex, but to actually provide kids with various contraception devices to reduce the incidence of pregnancy and venereal diseases.

Give New Emphasis to Training

Training conducted in the traditional fashion is quite
unproductive in creating actual change in the way
things are really done.

—LAWRENCE M. MILLER

In 1984, IBM spent nearly $700 million, or more than 1
percent of its gross receipts, on training and development.
During that same year, a large school district with a budget
of almost $500 million spent less than $80,000 on such
training activities. At IBM, all managers are required to
undergo ninety hours of training each year. At this school
district, administrators are not required to undergo any
training. It does not take a genius to determine which organization is truly committed to its people, is sensitive to their
needs, is attempting to deal with obsolescence, is bent on
achieving excellence, really believes that its people are its
greatest asset.

It is time our public schools take a good look at what the
best-run companies in the United States are doing in terms
of training and development.

The Best-Run Companies Take Training Seriously

The best-run companies hold a common belief that in
order to remain competitive and to have an ample supply of

93

qualified people they must grow their own. To perform this feat, they provide on-the-job training as well as special courses, workshops, and seminars. Many have even established their own universities or training centers.

3M has several types of career training programs for its people. For its salespersons, there are special sales training programs. For its technical people, the company has a technical society that invites Nobel scientists to speak. And for its marketing personnel, 3M has a Marketing Director's Council that brings in nationally known marketing experts. Key managers are sent to headquarters for training. In addition, the company provides on-the-job training as well as special courses.

Knight-Ridder Newspapers Institute of Training is the industry's only college-accredited training and management development program. The Institute has its own training staff and forty-eight leaders. Since the Institute was founded in 1968, more than three thousand managers and other personnel have taken at least one of its seminars, and the number of seminars offered has grown from one to twenty-three. These seminars are designed to make well-rounded leaders out of individuals brought up through the ranks of the company. The program is so well thought of that 362 managers from other companies have paid to attend.

Universities established by the best-run companies include McDonald's University, Levi-Strauss University, Dana University, and Apple University. The curricula of these universities have been designed around the short-and long-range needs of both the companies and their people. Procter & Gamble maintains that the best training is on-the-job training provided by managers through direct personal communication, guidance, direction, and coaching, and therefore it has established a Corporation Supervisory Training Program to accommodate most of its training needs. The company uses this program to further its goal of ensuring that every employee makes a contribution and grows in his or her responsibilities.

Supplementing this on-the-job training are high-quality organized workshops, seminars, and other programs which are available to all company employees. The following statement by Robert V. Goldstein, vice president of advertising, provides evidence of P&G's commitment to training: "We must take the steps necessary to see that no one is denied exposure to these supplemental training opportunities because of the always pressing business needs of the moment. We simply can't permit people who have agreed to attend a long-planned training event to cancel their participation at the last moment because a pressing business matter can't wait an hour or two."

Two other best-run companies that have strong training programs are General Electric and IBM. GE conducts degree programs in conjunction with universities and maintains a thirty-acre training estate where over 5,000 GE people get training every year. During any given year, approximately 50 percent of all GE people are enrolled in some form of company-paid training and development program. IBM's management training and development program began in 1956 when Thomas Watson, Jr., the son of IBM's founder, asked one of its managers, Tom Clemans, to solve the problem of finding top managers by establishing a training center. This center is located at the company's headquarters in Armonk, New York. Many of the training seminars held there are conducted by some of the most distinguished scholars in the academic world.

John Young, president of Hewlett-Packard, whose views echo those of most of the best-run companies, maintains that " 'Growing our own people' results in a strong upward flow of supervisors and managers knowledgeable not only in terms of their profession, but also the company and its business. This is a very important requirement if we are going to fulfill the promise of management by objectives, because once that principle has been set into action, it can only carry on if everyone in the organization understands it and works at it."

At Control Data, nearly every facility has its own training center, and one of these has a battery of Plato computer terminals to accommodate the company's numerous individualized computerized courses. All managers and most engineers are required to take a minimum of forty hours of training a year. In 1982, Control Data managers spent an average of forty-seven hours in training, of which 70 percent was on the Plato computers. That year, company managers received a total of a quarter of a million hours of training. These figures do not include additional training which the managers may have acquired on their own by attending outside seminars and conferences. Other Control Data employees received an additional million hours of training.

Our Schools Must Grow Their Own

Assuming responsibility for growing our own school people has never been a strong feature of the public education system in this country. Boards of education as well as school administrators tend to believe that once a person has received formal education through undergraduate and graduate courses he or she is well prepared to tackle teaching and school administration. How far this is from the truth! Formal education merely provides a theoretical basis and a limited amount of practical experience, which should serve as the foundation for further training by the school district.

School districts must look upon each new school person in terms of his or her potential for training and development. They must provide opportunities for ongoing training, and they must motivate each individual person to participate actively in the training and development program.

An essential aspect of a commitment to training and development is the allotment of adequate funds. The board of education and superintendent must understand that a sound and comprehensive training and development program is imperative, and must back this understanding with appropriate budget allocations. An adequate budget allocation for training and development is 1 percent of the school district's yearly budget. If a school district's budget is $25 million, then the training budget should be a minimum of $250,000. If the board of education does not want to increase the training budget to this level in one year, it may do so gradually over three years—i.e., by allotting .05 percent the first year, .08 percent the second year, and 1 percent the third year.

A second vital ingredient is the allocation of personnel—most importantly, the naming of the individual who will be responsible for training and development. Usually training and development is a unit within the human resources or personnel department. However, if a school district is really interested in giving new emphasis to training and development, this responsibility perhaps should be assigned to an assistant superintendent.

Once a school district has made an adequate commitment to training and development by allotting funds and allocating personnel, there are a number of ways in which training activities can be developed and implemented. Following are some considerations that should be taken into account:

- A decision by a board of education or superintendent to build a training center or to convert an unused building for training purposes will communicate a clear message not only to school people but to all stakeholders that the school district is committed to "growing its own." This center should be established to train all school people regardless of position, status, and seniority, thus helping to create a family-like climate within the district. The best location for on-the-job training is as close to the central administration office as possible, and, with the exception of on-the-job training, all training and development activities should be done here. Within the center there should be rooms of a variety of sizes in order to accommodate individualized learning, mini-seminars, and small-, medium-, and large-group instruction. In addition, there should be computer rooms for data processing training, a large instructional media center with computer-controlled televisions, and, located throughout the center, individual carrels with and without electronic and computerized components.

- A decision by a board of education or superintendent to build a training center or to convert an unused building for training purposes will communicate a clear message not only to school people but to all stakeholders that the school district is committed to "growing its own." This center should be established to train all school people regardless of position, status, and seniority, thus helping to create a family-like climate within the district. The best location for on-the-job training is as close to the central administration office as possible, and, with the exception of on-the-job training, all training and development activities should be done here. Within the center there should be rooms of a variety of sizes in order to accommodate individualized learning, mini-seminars, and small-, medium-, and large-group instruction. In addition, there should be computer rooms for data processing training, a large instructional media center with computer-controlled televisions, and, located throughout the center, individual carrels with and without electronic and computerized components.

- School districts should have a strong orientation component to their training activities. As Harry Levinson says in the *Exceptional Executive*, ". . . the need for closeness is most crucial at the beginning of a relationship with an organization. It is at this point that people become 'attached,' and the attaching process must take place at a time when they are more confused about the new job and the strange organization." The orientation program of a school district should cover the school district's history, its current programs, its statement of philosophy, and how each school person is expected to contribute to its success. Orientation programs are an important part of the training and development activities at all of the best-run companies. In fact, such programs are considered so important that at many of these companies the top managers, including the CEO, are heavily involved. Unfortunately, at present most superintendents do not get involved in their school district's orientation programs, except perhaps to make a brief appearance at a session.

- Because of the wide disparity in the ability of newly hired teachers to teach, I recommend that no new teachers be assigned to the classroom until they have been trained in and demonstrated certain entry-level skills. With excellent selection and recruitment policies and a strong training and

NYACK COLLEGE MANHATTAN

development program, new teachers should be ready to teach in the classroom with some degree of excellence in no more than five months. An assessment of the strengths and weaknesses of each teacher will dictate at what point on the career path he or she should enter the training program. Much of the training should be conducted in the classroom setting under the tutelage of a mentor, with a variety of other training and development experiences supplementing the classroom instruction.

- A school district's training activities should include training in teamwork and team building. Areas that should be covered should include group dynamics, conflict resolution, problem solving, and how to be an effective self-manager and team manager.

- One component of any training program should be attitude training, designed to help school people reach an understanding and appreciation of the philosophy, code of conduct, and climate of the organization, as well as of the leadership style of the school administrators and supervisors.

- Training should be performed by the director of training, by principals, and by team leaders. Training by the director of training should consist primarily of classroom instruction related to competencies in a specific path. Training by principals should involve instructing team leaders on how to create cohesive teams and how to achieve the goals and objectives of the school district. Training by team leaders should consist of assisting team members to plan and control the instructional process.

- Training should focus directly on the behavior school people will be expected to exhibit immediately upon returning to the work environment. If school people participate in the training with a clear understanding that they will be expected to apply what they have just learned, their attitude toward the training will be markedly improved. Of course, school people will be much more open to training in any case if the training relates directly to their work situation. Making sure the training is relevant to the competencies to be mastered and to the job situation is the responsibility of the training director.

- Training should be performed in teams. When school people receive training on an individual basis, they generally feel that they are being requested to deviate from the norms of the group. When they are trained as a team, group psychology works to support the desired behavior.

- Any single program should be restricted to a reasonable period of time. Ideally a training program should consist of two-hour sessions once a week over a period of weeks. Training should not last for more than three consecutive days.

- All training should include an action component. Trainees should be required first to plan how they are going to execute the competencies learned during the training, and then to implement their plans in the actual work situation.

- All training should include some form of assess-

101

ment. Before a training program is completed, all trainees should be evaluated to determine to what extent the competencies covered have been mastered. Once the evaluation has been completed, the training director should review the results with the school person, pointing out areas needing improvement. For example, Andy Grove, president of People Express, maintains that his teaching role in the company's orientation program is one of his most important duties, and all the airline's senior-level managers are required to devote between four and eight hours per week to training new people.

- I believe it was Alfred North Whitehead who said that we can no longer rely on traditional methods to solve complex problems; thus, the training director should seek innovative methods to make training more meaningful to school people and the school district. One such innovative training program has been adopted by the Roosevelt School District on Long Island, New York. Under this program, co-sponsored by the school district and the University of Massachusetts, the school district pays the tuition of school people pursuing their doctorates as long as their course work and dissertations are related to the needs of the school district. A recent assessment indicates that the program has been well received by school people and that certain long-standing problems within the district are being worked on.

Because a new emphasis on training within a school district demonstrates to school people that the district not only cares about them but trusts them, morale should be boosted.

As a result, school people will be inspired to become more than they ever hoped to be, and the school district will find that promotion from within will become the rule rather than the exception.

I am reminded of a sorrowful story told to me by an administrator. When the assistant superintendent for personnel saw a director reading a how-to book on management prior to the superintendent's cabinet meeting, he commented, "If you have time to read a book you must not have enough to do; I must see to it that you get more work." Although this central administrator's attitude may not be representative of that of all school administrators, I do believe it is far too typical. School administrators must understand that in order to keep the school district in forward motion, they must continue their own learning. If they fail to continue their own learning through varied training and development activities, it will be almost impossible for them to nurture the kind of school environment necessary for achieving and sustaining excellence.

James O'Toole, author of *Vanguard Management*, is a strong proponent of this point of view. He states, "In general, the managers of the Vanguard are constantly reading and rereading, questioning, thinking, rethinking their most basic assumptions; willing, in short, to unlearn things that had led to past success but are likely to be anachronistic in the future. In fact, if I were forced to pick just one characteristic that distinguishes the Vanguard from the Old Guard, it would be openness to learning."

Strategies for Achieving Excellence

- Rather than sending just two or three people to a conference, send twenty or thirty. For example, if the school district is interested in adopting the quality circle concept, a group rather than a few individuals should be sent for appropriate training.

- Do what Hewlett-Packard, W. L. Gore & Associates, and People Express have done—use career mazes rather than the traditional career path program. Loosely defined "career mazes" give people the opportunity to develop multiple skills. As a result, people get training in those skills and areas which best fit their needs and interests. These career mazes are designed not to equip people to climb to the top, but to help them make a personal contribution and also make them more content with the company.

- Retain a professional writer to produce training materials. The fact that a school administrator has advanced degrees does not mean that he or she can communicate effectively for training and development purposes.

- Orient the actual training and development of school people around a concept I call "performance training." There are four steps in performance training: (1) analyzing the performance problem, (2) identifying appropriate competencies, (3) requiring the participants to perform the specific skills involved, (4) conducting follow-up training through situation assessments, correction, and repeated practice of the desired skills.

- Visit the following best-run companies to observe their training and development facilities and programs:

  –IBM

    –Dana Corporation
    –Apple Computer
    –General Electric
    –Control Data Corporation
    –Procter & Gamble

- Make certain all administrators receive adequate training in human relations skills, technical skills, and conceptual skills.

- Include, in addition to on-the-job training, the following training activities:

      –in-school workshops
      –team development meetings
      –advisory sessions
      –verification sessions
      –outside meetings and conferences
      –distribution of published materials

- Encourage principals to augment the training programs by:

      –providing mini-workshops to explain a function or activity
      –initiating think sessions to assist teams in solving problems
      –calling on specialists or experts to tutor a team member or team
      –initiating a mentorship program for individuals experiencing on-the-job problems
      –making arrangements for teams to participate in exchange programs

- Prepare a ten-year career-path strategic plan which contains:

–a forecast of socioeconomic conditions affecting
the school district
–a forecast of organizational needs
–a study of school people's goals
–a long-term budget
–a training activities agenda
–a description of how performance evaluation will
be conducted

- Train school people interested in being promoted
by:

    –Assigning them to assist a central administrator
    for a short period of time. This experience will
    provide a person with a broader view of the school
    organization, and thus is especially useful in
    training central administrators.
    –Giving them a special assignment.
    –Assigning them to perform a particular function
    in a project. (The essential difference between a
    special assignment and a project is that a special
    assignment is of brief duration whereas a project
    assignment lasts until the job is completed.)
    –Giving them additional responsibilities that pro-
    vide the kinds of experiences indicated in the
    career path plan.
    –Assigning them to a succession of different jobs in
    the school district. (During each of these rota-
    tional assignments, the person should perform all
    the duties associated with the job so that he or
    she acquires an in-depth knowledge of that func-
    tion.)

- Emulate Levi Strauss. The annual merit evaluation of managers is based in part on how well they
train their people. Each manager is expected to
cross-train a minimum of two people each year and

to act as mentor for one younger employee. Also as part of its training program, the company has established "training jobs," jobs which allow managers to receive lateral "promotions" so that they can increase their skills while they wait for a vertical promotion.

- Require that each school set aside an amount equal to between 1.4 percent and 10 percent of each employee's salary to be used for training.
- Develop a policy similar to that of Levi Strauss concerning how much training administrators are required to do, and base a large part of the performance evaluation of school administrators on the degree to which they train and develop school people.

Develop a training curriculum that meets the strategic concerns of the school district, and hold the training director responsible for ensuring that this training curriculum is used to train school people.

- Evaluate your district's present efforts to make itself a learning institution for school people as well as students, through use of training and development activities. Use the following questions along with others of your own choosing to develop a questionnaire for this purpose:

  –Is there a budget allocation specifically for training?
  –Does the school district have a formally designated training center?
  –Does the school district have a catalog of training programs and is it disseminated to all school people?
  –Does the training curriculum meet the cultural and strategic needs of the school district?

–Is the training director evaluated on how much school people's behavior changes after each training session?

Make Sure Superintendents Are Generalists

> We are moving from the specialist who is soon obsolete to the generalist who can adapt.
>
> —JOHN NAISBITT

A mistake often made by school districts when selecting a superintendent is to promote or hire a central administrator who has done extremely well in a specialized area—personnel, business administration, curriculum and instruction, or research and evaluation. What usually happens when such an administrator becomes a superintendent of schools is that he or she tends to continue practicing his or her specialty as before. This is only natural; the new superintendent, after all, is very familiar with the specialty, enjoys it, and knows what to do. The question is whether an administrator with such a limited perspective is able to lead his or her staff in effectively administering all operational areas of the school district.

Today there is a growing consensus in industry that the higher managers rise in an organization and the higher they wish to rise, the more important it is that they become familiar with many different operational areas of the company. Since there is very little difference in how a school district and how a business should be managed, it is my belief that school administrators who aspire to become superintendents of schools should also be generalists. This assertion is not construed to degrade those administrators who desire to specialize. All school districts need specialists, and in fact many central administrators are specialists by nature and would be unhappy in a generalist's position. But the demands of managing today's school districts, particularly those wishing to achieve excellence, require someone at the top who has had a macroscopic view of the overall organization, acquired through two or three years of hard experience in many different areas.

The Best-Run Companies Train Managers to Be Generalists

Training managers to be generalists is a tradition in many of the best-run companies. During his reign as CEO of IBM from 1956 to 1971, Tom Watson, Jr. established a rotation program in which managers were moved around and tested in new areas. In fact, the only specialists hired at that time who are still practicing their specialties are lawyers and outstanding scientists. All other managers were required to become capable in more than one discipline in order to get promoted. One of those managers is John Opel, who was rotated to twenty different areas or assignments before he became chairman of the board of IBM.

John W. Hanley, who was CEO of Monsanto Company in the 1970s, put into practice a well-conceived management training program and rotation plan through which a group of senior managers were trained to become integrated (my term) managers. Hanley put so much emphasis on this program that he personally interviewed each of the managers in the group and traveled extensively with them to observe their management style, behavior, strengths, and weaknesses.

At Delta Air Lines, most people perform a variety of jobs. This cross-utilization not only maximizes productivity but also gives employees an opportunity to learn new skills and to acquire an appreciation for the challenges experienced by other people. As a result of this cross-utilization policy, everyone at Delta knows that he or she has a shot at supervisory and management positions, even the position of president and chief operating officer. Ronald W. Allen, who is presently president and CEO, was rotated or promoted nine times in the twenty years before he assumed his present position.

Managers at Southern California Edison Company who desire to get ahead are encouraged to make lateral movements. As a result, sixteen corporate managers who constitute the company's executive management team have all worked in a variety of fields and areas.

Train Administrators to Be Generalists

The best way for school districts to ensure that they are or will be headed by superintendents who are generalists is for them to have their own succession programs, which give administrators experience in many different areas. Current superintendents must be the prime movers in instituting such programs. One of the most important functions of the school administrator is to provide continuity in the quest for excellence, and one important component of this task is developing and training a cadre of general school administrators who are capable of assuming the position of area or district superintendent. In effectively training others, superintendents contribute to their own development, as well as that of the people they train, as sensitive and caring educational leaders.

The following are some tips for the school district that has made a commitment to growing its own school administrators:

- Develop and implement a policy of hiring young school administrators who can do more than fulfill the minimum requirements of their job and who have the potential to become central administrators in ten to fifteen years. The school district will need to become proficient in predicting what its needs will be in the future so that potential general administrators can be identified accurately.

- Establish a career path program for each potential general administrator. This program should be designed to meet both the long-range general administration needs of the school district and the individual needs of the administrator. As the administrator progresses, the program should be modified in order to address strengths and weaknesses revealed by performance evaluations. The overall goal of each program is to enable administrators to

  –acquire a broad-based knowledge of the school organization
  –develop good relationships with a broad spectrum of school people
  –think more systematically about themselves and their own careers so that they can evaluate their own development and determine areas in need of improvement
  –look at issues, situations, and events more macroscopically

- Include in each potential administrator's career path program at least one to two years of hard experience in the areas of business administration, human resources, curriculum and instruction, and general administration. This means that potential

112

administrators should have a minimum of four years of experience to be eligible for the position of area or district superintendent. (Approximately two years ago, when I was conducting a workshop on Theory Z for a group of superintendents in Boston, I proposed to the group that school administrators be trained prior to being given the position of superintendent; they almost revolted. A lot of work will be required to take this particular step toward excellence.)

- Place young school administrators in jobs that are appropriate for them. This often involves more than placing a new administrator in a vacated position; it may involve specially designing a position or structuring assignments in the central administration office to fit a new administrator's characteristics and experience.

  In rotating administrators from job to job, special attention should also be paid to timing. If administrators are rotated to another assignment too soon, they may not have acquired proficiency in certain important skills. On the other hand, if too much time elapses before their next assignment, they may become bored and may look elsewhere for another position. Thus it is extremely important for the superintendent to become actively involved in the progress of each administrator.

- Provide opportunities for formal education at colleges or universities. (Unfortunately, I don't know of any educational administration school that offers a formal program in general school administration. Our colleges and universities would do well to develop such a program by emulating some of the programs offered by business schools to help managers become more problem-solving oriented, and more aware of a wide variety of issues, possibilities and ideas. Columbia University offers a unique course in its business school program in which a manager in business presents to the class a problem that his or her company is facing. After hearing all background information and relevant data, the class is divided into teams, each of which must, over the course of a month, analyze the problem and devise a solution. The solutions are presented to the manager, who critiques each one and then describes what the company actually did or plans to do. After the manager's presentation, the students are given the opportunity to present their views of the company's solution.

- Keep an eye out for those administrators-in-training who exhibit what John P. Kotter of the Harvard Business School calls "success syndromes." These administrators will have performed well in their previous assignments, and their success will have enhanced their self-esteem and motivation as well as their relationships with other administrators and their formal and informal power. Their successful performance will also have increased their interpersonal and intellectual skills. These are the administrators who promise to make the best superintendents.

Revamp the Present Method

Once a school district decides to grow its own superintendents, it will take three to five years to plan and implement a good succession program. What should be done in the meantime if a superintendent must be hired? I recommend that the following steps be taken in hiring a new superintendent from outside the district. Throughout the selection process, the people included should keep in mind that the school district is looking for a generalist.

- With the help of a consultant, the board should choose a team consisting of one retired and one active superintendent and two professors, one from a school of education and the other from a business college. This team should screen the submitted applications and resumes to select about ten candidates. In screening the applications, the team should ask the following questions:

  –Does the applicant have a terminal degree? (The answer to this question will indicate how serious the applicant is about his or her own education and training efforts.)
  –Are there indications that the applicant is a results-oriented proactive leader?
  –Is there evidence that the applicant is a godfather champion or an executive champion?
  –Has the applicant read such books as *In Search of Excellence, A Passion for Excellence, Creating Excellence,* or *Corporate Culture*?
  –Has the applicant ever attended courses in a business school?
  –Is the applicant familiar with such current topics as strategic planning, champions, entrepreneurship, Theory Z, soft and hard S's, egalitarianism, reverse feedback, career path planning, and succession planning?

- The consultant should administer personality and interest tests to each candidate to determine whether or not his or her personality and interests are compatible with the culture and needs of the school district. (In addition, I strongly recommend that the final two or three candidates be tested for brain-hemisphere dominance. The most effective superintendents have been shown to be those who are classified as L/R mode dominant, or integrated thinkers.)

- In order to reach a consensus on the final four candidates, members of the selection team should visit the school district in which each candidate presently works to get a feel for how good a manager the candidate is. The team should talk to board members, school people, and community members in that district; visit schools; attend meetings; and review plans, newsletters and memos.

- The final four candidates should be required to spend a week in the school district to prepare a strategic plan which should include a school district situation audit as well as five long-range goals and program strategies. The selection team should then evaluate and compare the proposals of the candidates and submit a written report of its findings, including a ranking of the candidates, to the board.

- The board should now establish a committee of school personnel and community members to interview the final candidates. After the candidates have been interviewed, the committee should discuss each candidate's strengths and weaknesses, and then the committee members should each put down on paper a ranking along with their reasons for the ranking. The consultant should review these rankings and report the collective outcome to the committee. This outcome should be discussed, and then the committee members should again each make another ranking. The collective outcome of this ranking, which should again be presented by the consultant to the committee, should be viewed as the committee's final ranking.

- Next, the board should review the various bits of information that have been collected about the candidates. These should include:

    –letters of application
    –resumes
    –written references
    –personality test results
    –interest test results
    –findings on brain-hemisphere dominance
    –findings of the selection team
    –the candidates' strategic plans
    –the final ranking of the candidates by the school personnel/community member committee.

- Finally, after conducting a four-hour interview with each finalist, the board should use the consensus process in making a final selection.

Strategies for Achieving Excellence

- Send for copies of the succession programs of the following best-run companies and use them to prepare your own programs:

    –IBM
    –Procter & Gamble

–Exxon
–Delta Airlines
–Knight-Ridder

- Identify two or three promising school administrators, determine whether they are interested in being trained as general administrators, and if so, move them out of their present positions if these positions are not conducive to growth.

- Establish a strict rule that all central administrators must become trained and educated in more than one discipline even if they are not interested in becoming superintendents.

- Become a mentor to two or three likely succession prospects.

- Follow the example of Security Pacific Corporation and Burroughs Corporation—require that all top-level managers (i.e., all central administrators and school principals) identify two or three potential successors for their jobs and meet with these people to set up a training and development program. Institute a practice of having the superintendent and board president (or board) meet annually to review the grooming progress of each potential successor.

Hints for Achieving Excellence

Breakthrough changes that help a company attain a
higher level of performance are likely to reflect the
interplay of a number of smaller changes.
                                    —ROSABETH MOSS KANTER

Although some of these hints come from my vast collec-
tion of books, magazines, articles, and papers, many of them
originated in my own experiences as a teacher, school
administrator, superintendent of schools, college professor,
and lifelong student trying to fulfill my purpose in life. I am
offering you only those hints which have proven to be successful in achieving results. Although most of these hints
can be implemented within a brief period of time, a few take
longer. Before any of the long-range hints are implemented,
you are advised to do further study in order to develop an
effective and comprehensive implementation plan. Some
hints are subtle in nature, and are intended to give you food
for thought. I have only included hints for boards of education, superintendents and principals, because it is on the
supervisory levels that change must begin if we are to
achieve excellence in our schools.

Board of Education:

- A board of education should not be apologetic
  when it spends funds for its members to go to con-
  ventions, visit schools, or attend workshops, even

119

if the expenditure exceeds the category allocation. These educational endeavors serve as a reward for services rendered, as well as a means of updating the board members' knowledge base, which will in turn help them to make better decisions.

- A board should make sure it has done everything possible in terms of hiring minority and female school personnel. A board that has hired minorities only in the areas of physical education and music, for example, may be considered racist.

- A board that has not adopted standards for evaluating student achievements, student and employee absenteeism, and the district's fiscal health is not performing in a satisfactory manner.

- A school district that does not have a strategic plan is going nowhere.

- A board president who contacts the superintendent more than three times a week is acting more as an administrator than as a board member and should rethink his or her role.

- An effective practice for improving board meetings is for the president and the superintendent to meet no later than one day after every meeting in order to critique the strengths and weaknesses of the meeting and reach a mutual understanding as to where improvements can be made.

- A board that takes less than four hours to assess the performance of the superintendent needs some training in evaluation.

- A board should evaluate its superintendent on the extent to which he or she holds principals and other administrators accountable.

- A board that turns down more than 5 percent of the superintendent's recommendations regarding personnel is being too "political" and is not acting in the best interests of the school district. If a superintendent is prevented from hiring the team members he or she chooses because of the political considerations of members of the board of education, he or she cannot be held accountable and responsible for the success or failure of the school district.

- A board that retains a dysfunctional superintendent because it can control him or her is not interested in achieving excellence and is doing a disservice to the school district. What should the board members do? Resign.

- To improve its effectiveness, a board of education should request that the superintendent evaluate the performance of each board member and the board as a whole and present reasons for his or her evaluation. Unfortunately, far too many boards are unwilling to let the person most affected by their performance conduct this "reverse feedback."

- A board member who allows himself or herself to be intimidated by either a member of the community or a school person into voting in a certain way is useless and should resign.

- A board of education should think twice about hiring consultants to help it select a superintendent. Many consultants have their own network of people, and sometimes it is difficult for excellent candidates to get into this "circle"; many consultants charge too much for what they do; many consultants are not fortified with new theories and prac-

121

tices regarding the management of people; and, finally, the most important reason—school districts should establish a strong training and development program and should "grow their own."

- A board of education should encourage its superintendent to keep abreast of developments in education by traveling about the country for a week or so every year looking at other school districts, seeing what other superintendents, principals, and teachers are doing, and searching for innovative programs, policies, and procedures that these districts have implemented in order to achieve excellence.

- A board has an obligation to advise community members as to when it is proper to address an issue being considered by the board and when it is not. A community member should never be permitted to interrupt the formal proceedings of board meetings. Questions and comments from the audience should be saved until the meeting is opened to the public.

- There is a direct correlation between the number of board meetings held monthly and the effectiveness of the board. The formula is simple: the greater the number of meetings above two, the more ineffective the board is. The need for more rather than fewer meetings indicates that the board is indecisive and is delving too much into the administrative responsibilities of the superintendent.

- A board that examines every single item in the budget does not trust its school superintendent.

- Boards should stop consuming numerous hours discussing items not directly related to the education of kids and use the time to concentrate on how students are educated.

- Boards should make arrangements to receive fifteen to twenty minutes of training in a specific subject during each working meeting.

Superintendent:

- One of the responsibilities of a superintendent is to train a central administrator to be his or her successor; he or she should begin doing so immediately upon assuming the position.

- A school district's orientation program should last no less than four weeks. It should contain information about the school district, its history and successes, its management style, and how each school within the district relates to the others. In essence, the orientation program should show new people how all school people work together to make things happen and how their individual role fits into the larger picture.

- The worst mistake a superintendent can make is not planning; the next worst is not doing so on a long-range basis.

- When hiring school administrators, a superintendent should place less emphasis on position competence and more on human relations skills, good reasoning ability, independent thinking, self-starting traits, and controlled aggressiveness.

- One of the biggest farces in public education is the superintendent's one-day in-service program. Reason: Nothing usually occurs as a result of the day's activities.

- A superintendent should give teaching team members the responsibility for selecting any new teachers who will be assigned to their teams.

- A superintendent should include representatives of the appropriate unions in all discussions that affect unionized school employees.

- A superintendent should have a policy that any school district employee can visit him or her without a prior appointment.

- A superintendent should assess his or her own strengths and weaknesses and select assistants whose abilities will be complementary.

- School districts should be allowed to experiment and make mistakes in order to find new directions for achieving excellence.

- A superintendent should use power reverently, with rewards instead of authoritative or coercive power.

- A superintendent should recognize and reward at least one person each day.

- A superintendent should have a record of and acknowledge the birthdays of all school people.

- A superintendent should make an effort to personally greet all new school people when they first arrive in the school district.

- One of the chief assets of excellent superintendents is their ability to spot and attract talented people.

- When implementing participative management, a superintendent should consider starting a school management newsletter to help both principals and teachers to understand their respective roles.

- A superintendent should periodically take time to eat in the cafeteria with groups of teachers and ask them about their concerns and needs. The teachers may be skeptical at first; they may need some time to become acclimated to this new practice.

- A superintendent should never take more than a month to hire a school person. If an employee is good, other school districts will also be looking to hire him or her.

- During the recruitment process, the chief responsibility of a superintendent is to market the school district or himself or herself in order to make the applicant want to become a member of the staff.

- A superintendent who makes no effort to organize his or her central administrators into an effective team is doomed to fail.

- Before selecting a personal computer, a superintendent should hire a consultant.

- A superintendent should prepare for board meetings by going over each item on the agenda, anticipating what questions will be asked by both board and community members, and hearing and reacting to the individual presentations of participating central administrators.

- Whenever an irate parent tries to initiate an argument at a public meeting, a superintendent should remain silent, because objective discussion at that moment is impossible.

- A superintendent should never turn his or her back on an irate parent.

- Maintaining a computerized book inventory will save money.

- A superintendent who does nothing when he or she learns that principals are not evaluating teachers' performance is negligent.

- A superintendent should require that each principal appear before an annual meeting of the central administration to announce what goals and objectives were and were not achieved during the year, indicate reasons in the cases where goals were not achieved, and discuss what actions will be taken to make improvements. The principal should also cite any awards or other forms of recognition received by either students or staff and present any ideas he or she has for the future benefit of students.

- IBM requires that all managers undergo ninety hours of training each year. School districts should require at least this amount.

- A superintendent should consider giving school administrators time off to work on a worthy project in the community.

- A school district should establish a college or training center called something like The Omni School District College or The Omni School District Training Center.

- If funds are not a problem, a superintendent should hire both a public relations specialist and a marketing expert. If funds are limited, the marketing expert should be hired.

- No school personnel should be fired unless a committee of administrators can reach a consensus over the dismissal. Reason: This system will prevent principals from firing teachers who have not received the proper guidance and direction from their principals. I have known of far too many able non-tenured teachers who were fired because principals failed to coach them correctly.

- A superintendent should establish a special fund to which local individuals, groups, and companies can contribute in order to support those activities of excellence which cannot be funded by the general budget.

- At Christmas, a superintendent should give time off to school people so that they can collect food and toys for needy parents of the community. The special fund can be used for substitutes.

- A superintendent should include union presidents in his or her cabinet.

- To expeditiously inculcate a statement of philosophy, a superintendent should determine its important values and organize them into a document called something like "Newton's Twenty-Five

Thoughts." Some examples of appropriate values are involving teachers in decision making; recognizing and rewarding good performance; being professional at all times; using mistakes as learning opportunities; etc. After the document has been discussed at length with all employees, it should be posted in a conspicuous place in all schools and used for training purposes.

- A superintendent should eliminate all administrative perks. Reason: Districts that are egalitarian are more likely to achieve excellence.

- A superintendent should seek administrators who are coaches, team builders, and expanders of people.

- A non-tenured teacher whose attendance rate is below 96.5 percent (the nation's average) should not be granted tenure. A tenured teacher whose attendance rate is below 96.5 percent should not be granted a salary increment.

- A superintendent should start a wellness program for school people, using school nurses or home economists or members of the physical education staff as instructors.

- In order to select a method of instruction for students preparing to take the SAT, a superintendent should conduct an experiment. Two similar groups of tenth and eleventh grade students should be established. In-school instruction should be arranged for one of the groups, and instruction by a commercial SAT preparatory firm for the other. When the test results come out, the SAT scores of both groups should be analyzed; if there is a significant difference, the school district should go with the method that produces the best results.

- Only a gutless superintendent is reluctant to rotate a not-so-excellent principal to another position. Which is more important, the temporary loss of self-esteem of an administrator or the loss of crucial years of learning by students?

- A school person who uses up all of his or her sick days for incidental reasons for five consecutive years is abusing the sick leave plan and should be informed that charges may be brought if his or her attendance record does not improve.

- All superintendents should protect themselves by explicitly citing in their contract the conditions of their employment—i.e., the goals and objectives that should be achieved, how progress toward their achievement will be measured, how problems will be resolved, the areas in the school district needing major improvement, how central administrative teams will be hired, the techniques that will be used for reviewing and reporting the performance of both individual board members and the board as a whole.

- A superintendent should conduct periodic "talk back to the superintendent" meetings.

- A superintendent should periodically teach a class within the school district and should insist that all non-teaching professionals do likewise.

- A superintendent should hold an annual "State of the School District" meeting with school personnel and community members in either January or May. At the meeting, the superintendent should describe goals and objectives that have been achieved as well as objectives, issues and problems that need to be worked on. He or she should also address concerns of members of the audience. There should be refreshments, and high-achieving school people should be recognized and rewarded.

- When in doubt about the morale of the school district, the superintendent should conduct a climate study of each school and take whatever actions are indicated.

- A superintendent who understands the importance of infusing a comprehensive training program within the school year will establish both a teaching school calendar and a professional school calendar. The teaching school calendar will indicate when students should be in attendance at school; the professional school calendar will indicate when all professional staff should be in attendance.

- A superintendent should try to hold on to high achievers by increasing their authority and responsibility.

- A superintendent should establish a goal with respect to promotions—for example, within three years three highly competent persons within the school district will be promoted.

- A superintendent should keep an eye out for how principals treat their school champions. Reason: One of the worst things that can happen to a superintendent is for the school district to lose its school champions because administrators do not treat them well.

130

- Getting references in writing is quite often not a reliable way to check on an applicant. A better way is to obtain a reference through a personal meeting or telephone call.

- A superintendent (as well as other school people) should become an expert on a new subject every two years. For example, during my seven years as regional training director, I became an expert on quality circles, Theory Z, strategic planning, and staff absenteeism.

- A superintendent should give each administrator the responsibility of learning his or her supervisor's job.

- Once a board gets a negative attitude about a superintendent, it's time for him or her to resign. Reason: Attitudes are difficult to change, so unless there's going to be a substantial change in the composition of the board, things will only get worse.

Principal:

- The best resource for solving problems is teachers.

- Excellent principals practice the one-minute management approach by visiting every teacher each day for approximately one minute.

- A not-so-excellent principal will chastise teachers for making a mistake, whereas an excellent one will use the mistake as an opportunity for training and development.

- A principal should designate excellent teachers as mentors and assign them to show new teachers how things are done in the school.

- Giving students freedom without structure can be disastrous.

- Excellent principals treat each teacher as a unique individual, with particular wants and needs.

- Excellent principals make it a point to do some teaching in the classroom on a periodic basis.

- Even if the solutions arrived at by a principal are better, teachers will more enthusiastically implement those that they themselves come up with.

- An excellent principal feels personally responsible for the welfare of all of his or her people on and off the job.

- Before speaking with the superintendent about making a purchase or establishing a new program or procedure, a principal should consult with all school people who will be affected by the change and get their opinions. Only if opinions are favorable should a principal speak to the superintendent.

- An excellent principal is a firm believer in egalitarianism. Therefore, he or she is a firm believer in reducing rank distinctions, eliminating preferred parking areas, eliminating separate dining rooms for administrators, etc.

- Teamwork should begin the first day of school.

- A principal should always personally greet a returning absentee and indicate that he or she was missed.

- A principal should identify the teachers who are most frequently absent and concentrate on improving this group's absenteeism rate.

- A principal should visit the classrooms of all substitute teachers at least three times a day.

- It is almost impossible to have a well-disciplined class if student conduct in the halls is disorderly.

- A principal should insist that all school people address each other by their first names.

- A principal should look for opportunities to share power with teachers.

- A principal should work hard to maintain a family feeling in the school.

- An excellent principal is one who is willing to get out of the way of teachers and let them perform.

- From time to time, a principal should call teachers together, if only for a few minutes, to congratulate them.

- An excellent principal permits his or her teams to set their own objectives. Individual members of the team should also set their own objectives.

- An excellent principal practices "visible management."

- A principal should meet at least once every month with union representatives to keep them informed

133

of upcoming activities, school progress, concerns, issues, and problems.

- Organizing a school into teams and giving them a great deal of autonomy will usually make a principal's job easier, will improve teacher morale, and will enhance a principal's effectiveness.

- The best kind of performance evaluation is one in which a principal and teacher decide together on any areas needing improvement.

* LESSON 10 *

Recognize and Reward Excellence

Everyone has a need to be somebody, but oftentimes the sheer size of the organization prevents the individual from gaining the recognition he or she thrives on.
—GAR TRUSLEY

Historically, school administrators have been relatively negligent in recognizing and rewarding school people for jobs well done. I personally have run across numerous cases in point—a janitor who went unrecognized after devoting forty-seven years of service to a school district without a single absence, a principal who received an "Outstanding Administrator" award from a group in the community but did not receive any recognition from his superintendent, a newly appointed director of an urban school district who did not even receive a thank-you note after working until 2:00 a.m. to get out a report for the superintendent, and a secretary who never received any acknowledgment after working a full day on Saturday to complete some letters and a report for the principal.

When school superintendents and administrators take the trouble to be sensitive to the recognition needs of people, the response can be overwhelming. When I was superintendent in Massachusetts, I sent orchids to two teachers who had just completed a successful experimental teaching program. With tears rushing down her cheeks, one of the teachers told me that in her fourteen years of teaching, she had never before received a compliment from an administrator. She placed the orchid between two pages in a Bible. The intent of this lesson is not to chastise school administrators or to denigrate them for not recognizing feats of excellence, but to indicate what needs to be done. Perhaps we can get some help from the best-run companies in America.

The Best-Run Companies Reward a High Percentage of People

Both *In Search of Excellence* and *Passion for Excellence* report that the best-run companies advocate what is referred to as a "degree of winning" principle rather than a "degree of losing" one. As a result, these companies recognize and reward a high percentage of their people, usually from 10 to 60 percent, whereas not-so-excellent companies recognize and reward only from 1 to 3 percent of their people. The practice of rewarding as many people as possible is based on the idea that doing so encourages people to believe that they too can be part of a "winning circle" and therefore motivates them to achieve.

IBM gives a "Golden Circle" award to all sales people whose annual sales top one million dollars. In 1984, Golden Circle members and their spouses received an all-expenses-paid trip to Hawaii. In addition, IBM sponsors the One Hundred Percent Club as a means of recognizing the more than two-thirds of its sales persons who have achieved company goals.

Merle Norman Cosmetics recognizes and rewards its employees for perfect attendance. In 1982, fifty-four company people, or nearly one-tenth of all employees, were recognized for not missing a single day of work. Also recognized were twenty-one people who had worked more than five years and eight who had worked more than ten years without missing any time. The company offers the following gifts for perfect attendance:

One year:	A gold engraved watch
Two years:	An Atari video game, a Farberware cookware set, or Oneida stainless flatware
Four years:	A Sunbeam or Cuisinart food processor
Five years:	A Nikon camera
Six years:	A Panasonic AM/FM, stereo eight-track cassette player with two-way speakers
Seven years:	An RCA 17″ color TV
Eight years:	A Panasonic microwave oven
Nine years:	A specially designed ring
Ten years:	A two-week, all-expenses-paid trip to Hawaii for two
Fifteen years:	A two-week, all-expenses paid trip anywhere in the world.

Mary Kay Cosmetics holds an Annual Awards Night at the Dallas Convention Center which is attended by more than 8,000 of its salespersons. During this festive event, Mary Kay's people are recognized, applauded, praised, and provided with gifts such as pink Cadillacs, mink coats, and diamond rings. "Queens of Sales" are crowned and given flowers and scepters amid standing ovations and musical salutes.

Nissan Motor Manufacturing Corporation, U.S.A. has a program called the "Pay for Skills Program" whereby its people are rewarded for their ability to perform different jobs. (To acquire the necessary skills to perform the various jobs, they are provided time for training during the work day.)

At Nordstrom, a company which operates thirty-six fashion specialty stores, a Pacesetter Award is given to those persons who have exceeded their goals by a large margin. In

1982, twenty-five company people were admitted to the Pacesetters' Club. As a Pacesetter, an individual is given a certificate and a business card with the imprint "Pacesetter" and is entitled to invite a guest to a lavish evening of dining, dancing, and entertainment. In addition, Pacesetters receive a 33 percent discount on all Nordstrom merchandise.

Sometimes the recognition given to high-achieving people consists simply of a gesture of appreciation. At Intel, when a company person does an outstanding job, the founder calls him or her into his office, reaches into his desk, and gives the person a handful of M&Ms. And at Addison-Wesley Publishing Company, a bronze star is passed from one high achiever to another, and a company person who is up against a hard time is eligible to receive the "Martyr of the Week" award.

Actions Meriting Recognition and Reward

There are at least four important areas in which exemplary actions by school people should be recognized and rewarded.

First and most important, individuals, teams and schools should be recognized for making significant progress toward realizing long-range goals. Each long-range goal should be accompanied by a plan of progress, and school people who achieve on plan or better than plan should be rewarded according to a predetermined recognition and reward program. For example:

- If a school district has a long-range goal of improving reading scores, it should establish performance standards in reading for each year within the time frame of the long-range plan. At the end of each school year, both students who have achieved above standard and their teachers should be given an elaborate dinner as well as an award such as a pen. Those who have achieved above standard for three consecutive years might be made members of the "Golden Circle" and be given a gold ring, a certificate, and discount coupons for merchandise from local participating stores. In addition, every year, schools that are on target in meeting reading performance standards might receive a "Pacesetting School" plaque at a banquet honoring all students and personnel at that school. These people might also be given a badge that reads "I am a Pacesetter."

- If the school district has a long-range goal of substantially improving attendance rates, an honor roll that lists the names of all school people who had perfect attendance the previous year could be posted in the main office of each school. In addition, those who have had perfect attendance for, say, five years could be recognized at a banquet given in their honor and also awarded some kind of gift. School people who have had perfect attendance for more than five years could receive more lavish gifts, including money.

- School people who were responsible for getting grants that help the district reach its long-term goals should be recognized and rewarded. I instituted such a reward program when I was director of a regional training center: If a proposal for under $100,000 was approved, a large cake was purchased, along with cider. The title and the amount of the grant were inscribed on the cake, and one large candle was positioned in the middle. The person who did the most to help the associate director of development prepare the grant was entitled to blow out the candle. If a grant for more than $100,000 was approved, an elaborate hot meal was provided in addition to a cake. Board members were invited to attend these celebrations. During the year in which I first instituted this strategy, we received almost a million dollars in grants, and for one grant we were one of only six recipients chosen from a pool of 800 applicants.

Second, individuals, teams, or schools should be recognized and rewarded for the creation and implementation of innovative approaches to achieving excellence. For example, a school could be given an award for the successful adoption of a quality circle program.

Third, school people should be recognized for exemplary performance of a specific job or duty. Teachers whose students have improved the most academically, for example, should be rewarded. The rewards themselves could be a certificate of recognition, a free dinner, and a $500 savings bond. If a school district would like to encourage collective action, it could also give awards to schools in which both students and teachers met certain attendance standards. (An acceptable standard for student attendance is 94.5 percent and for school personal 96.5 or 98 percent.) The award for students could be a badge stating, "I am from a school with good attendance." Teachers could receive a certificate or some other form of recognition. At the end of the school year, the two groups could be entertained by a professional group as a joint reward for good attendance.

Finally, individuals, teams, and schools should be recognized and rewarded for showing a high degree of loyalty and teamwork. For example, a school district could reward the team that has displayed the most togetherness and/or individuals who have done the most in terms of team building.

Some Additional Pointers About Awards

- Establish multiple award programs whereby awards are given to the top 60 percent, 25 percent, 5 percent, and 1 percent of school people rather than to just a few. The point is to make as many people as possible winners.

- The best types of awards are small gifts or sums of money, letters of appointment, letters on personal stationery, public announcements, announcements at staff meetings, announcements in newsletters, certificates of completion, plaques, letters of congratulation, pins, luncheons, dinners, displays of projects, recreational activities, letters of congratulation to family members, and trips. Whatever the award, the same one should be given to all members of a team.

- An award does not have value unless it is given with conviction and for perceived merit.

- When considering instituting an awards program, get input from potential recipients as to standards for achieving awards.

Promotion is another effective management tool for recognizing and rewarding excellence. Many of the best-run companies, such as IBM, 3M, Procter & Gamble, Hewlett-Packard, and Publix Super Markets, are strong proponents of promoting from within.

In fact, these companies tie in their career path program with their policy of promoting from within. Although many school districts have been known to promote from within, more substance has to be given to this practice by offering a strong training and development program coupled with a career path program to give all people an equal chance for getting promoted. Promotion in school districts should not be something that happens as a matter of chance.

The human resources department is responsible for meeting with each school person and preparing a career path program. Each year these programs should be updated. In addition, the superintendent and board of education should periodically review the career path records of potential general school administrators and make suggestions and promotions as determined desirable. The human resources department should review the career path programs of other school people desiring to be transferred or promoted and keep tabs on their progress. From time to time, based upon observations and performance reviews, changes or modifications in the career path plans most likely will be necessary. The human resources department is accountable for supervising the career path program of all employees.

Community Reaction

One problem I foresee for school districts in establishing an effective recognition and reward program is reluctance on the part of both boards of education and superintendents to grant lucrative rewards because of uncertainty about how the community will react. True, there may be some members of the community who will object when they learn that a school person received an expensive gold watch for twenty-five years of perfect attendance, or that a team was awarded an all-expenses-paid "education tour" because of outstanding achievement in reading and math. This is to be expected; however, if a comprehensive effort is made to explain all aspects of the school district's attempt to achieve excellence, most community people will have few or no objections to satisfying school people's recognition needs.

At Bowman High School in Bowman, North Carolina, a number of changes were initiated to improve students' test scores. In addition, to get students mentally set to take the state's comprehensive test of basic skills, pep rallies and slogans were used, such as "Do your best in the CTBS." One class developed a poster reading: "Is your school low in morale? Well, the CTBS is the test to use. It will show your intelligence, smarts, and your charm. Doing good on this test won't bring you any harm. So do it for yourself and not for anybody else." The bottom of the poster included a drawing of Mr. T, saying, "I pity the fool who plays around with the CTBS Test!"

What was the impact of the school district improvement efforts and the hoopla activities? The results were 15 percent greater than the state required. When the principal announced the results of the test scores over the public address system, thunderous cheers resounded throughout the corridors of the school building.

Strategies for Achieving Excellence

- Institute an annual gala affair in which the school district celebrates the most productive teachers or school personnel.

- Hire a limousine to transport "The Top School Personnel" to school for an entire week. Arrange for the expenses to be paid for by a local business.

- Get the PTA to sponsor a weekend all-expenses-paid trip for the winner of the most productive teacher award and his or her spouse. The standards on which the award is based should be developed jointly by a task force of the school district and the PTA.

- Publish a quarterly magazine devoted exclusively to congratulating school personnel for outstanding accomplishments. The name of this magazine should be one that identifies its purpose, such Appreciation, Applause, Thank You, etc. The magazine should describe what individuals, teams, and schools have done to achieve excellence and contain numerous illustrations and photographs.

- Consider establishing an academic achievement recognition program. Because the thrust is to achieve improved results in schools through teams, the teams should receive the awards. The awards could consist of bronze, silver, and gold pins. Obviously, they should be handed out at a gala affair and be given a great deal of publicity.

- Consider adopting an appreciation program that Tom Peters and Nancy Austin call PEET, for "Program for Ensuring that Everybody's Thanked." Under this program, every Monday morning the members of the central administration team receive a PEET Sheet. This document lists three outstanding team leaders, what their teams are presently doing, and identifies the administrators who have visited the teams. This program not only helps in the recognition of top-performing teams but also encourages the practice of management by wandering around.

- Prepare and implement a short-range and long-range recognition and reward program tied to the school district's goals and objectives.

- Praise at least one outstanding achiever every day.

- Take a cue from Bernard Moore, principal of the Costley Middle School in East Orange, New Jersey. Each year he holds a breakfast or luncheon meeting in which recognition and plaques are awarded to the various team leaders as a token of his appreciation for a job well done.

- Make sure school people are recognized and complimented for jobs well done. School people should also be complimented for any out-of-school achievements, such as election to public office, or receipt of a civic award.

- Establish a "School of the Month" award as a means of publicly recognizing outstanding effort.

- Reward school people for outstanding deeds or for timely completion of projects by giving them additional training and development opportunities or some time off.

- Make sure to promote outstanding people.

- Give school people who achieve excellence inspirational gifts.

- Establish a school district "Hall of Fame" containing plaques with the names of high-achieving school people, accompanied by photographs and descriptions of their achievements.

• LESSON 11 •

Achieve Excellence Through Teams

Everything important in life happens as a result of teamwork or collective effort.

—WILLIAM OUCHI

It has been echoed over and over by the CEOs of the best-run companies that the two most common weaknesses of U.S. corporations are the failure to encourage teamwork and excessive management. This proclamation is no doubt also true of the school districts; and although excessive levels of management may not be a problem in small and medium-sized school districts, failure to organize school people into effective teams certainly is. What is needed is a major effort by all school districts to structure the entire school organization so as to foster team identity, team planning, team control, team problem solving, and team excellence. The greater use of teams and the acceptance of responsibility by these teams will in turn reduce the need for layers of management.

This lesson will focus on team organization and the team process; the roles of teams in schools will be considered in Lesson 12.

Bits and Pieces in the Best-Run Companies

Peters and Waterman use the name chunking to refer to the practice of dividing people into teams to facilitate organizational fluidity, and they refer to the teams themselves as bits and pieces. Over the years teams have also received such labels as task forces, project centers, quality circles, skunk works, and champions. They are usually the most visible part of the organization and are the building blocks of the best-run companies; however, they never show up on an organizational chart.

The best-run companies have found a number of different ways to organize and use teams. Control Data Corp. has established what is referred to as special work-force action teams, or SWATs, each composed of several employees who work for ninety days on jobs previously done by outside contractors. SWAT jobs usually consist of menial work such as painting, plumbing, and merging old files. CRS Sirrine, Inc. has used teams for years. Each team consists of six to eight architects who work on three to six different projects at a time. As a result, each team gets experience in various facets of the business. At Delco Remy, all employees are team members or support persons (all plant managers are support persons). Each team selects its own leader, and the line supervisor is the "team advisor." At weekly meetings, the team advisor presents the team's goals for the following week, and the team also deals with any problems, business or personal, brought up by team members. At General Mills, there are groups of teams; each team within the group works on a brand-name product. For example, the "Big 6" group has teams working on Cheerios, Wheaties, Trix, Kix, Nature Valley Granola and so forth. Each team is involved in all facets of making and selling that product, from production to advertising to distribution. 3M makes use of New Venture Teams. A New Venture Team is essentially a task force of volunteers who plan the production of a new product. If testing indicates that the product is likely to be a money-maker, a new division may be organized to produce it.

The best-run companies also use project teams to solve problems. When John Opel was CEO of IBM, he assembled a project team of experts whose efforts led to the development of IBM's personal computer. Other companies that use project teams include Boeing, Bechtel, and Fluor.

Western Electric has more than 15,000 of its people organized into permanent quality circles which do "skunk work"—that is, identification, analysis, and solving of unit-related problems. Many other companies use temporary quality circles, known as Tactical Action Teams, which are organized to solve a particular problem and then are abandoned.

R. G. Boerg Corporation, a footwear manufacturer, converted to a team process by organizing 300 employees into teams consisting of eight to twelve employees. Each team is responsible for the manufacturing of a specific product from the raw materials to the finished product. In addition, each team is allowed to participate in the company's overall decision-making activities. One employee's statement attests to the value of the team process: "Before, everyone was on his own and no one cared about helping his fellow employee. Now everyone is dependent upon everybody else. I know, in my case, I think twice before taking a day off, because I know if I do, it will affect my team."

Jerry Sanders, President of Advanced Micro Devices, Inc., has established what is one of the nation's finest management structures, and it is composed chiefly of teams. All people are identified as team members. Teams are led by a managing director and are organized around specific responsibilities, such as "The Quality Central Reviewing Inspection Team" and "Mail and Literature Distribution Team." Apple Computer, one of the most egalitarian companies in the United States, has organized all of its operations around teams. There is a general management team, an Apple II team, a MacIntosh team, a sales team, a creative team, and a human resources team. (Wouldn't it be wonderful if school districts would build their operations around similar teams, such as a central administration team, a human resources team, teaching teams, and support teams?)

Intel thinks so highly of teamwork and team building that it specifically mentions teams in its statement of philosophy. This statement reads in part: "Teams are an integral part of the Intel work ethic environment. Team performance is critical to the accomplishment of Intel objectives . . ..Team objectives take precedence over individual objectives. This principle is applied in day to day operations and is fundamental. If changes in job assignment or organizational structure are necessary, they are made in a manner to optimize team results, rather than to maintain individual career paths." Teams at Intel come in a variety of forms. There are formally defined teams, such as the Field Sales Force and Fab IV; special teams, called task forces, which are formed to solve major problems, many of which are interdivisional in nature; and "invisible" teams, which are not formally defined or specially formed, but organize spontaneously to solve problems that occur during normal operations. It is only through the efforts of these various teams that Intel achieves its aggressive objectives.

Parameters for Using Teams

What is a team? A team is basically two or more people who cooperate and coordinate their activities to achieve a common goal; are representative of important subsystems of an organization; have some degree of reciprocal influence over each other; and interact through a formal substructure.

When should teams be used? Even where an entire organization is organized into teams, there must be some parameters for using teams and not using them. Social-psychological research as well as the accumulated experience and wisdom of our best-run companies indicates that teams are particularly appropriate for

- increasing collaboration
- giving those who feel that they have something to offer an opportunity to get involved
- building consensus on controversial matters
- allowing those who are going to be affected by a decision to be represented in making that decision
- solving problems that belong to no identifiable party
- confronting vested interest groups in order to effect change
- dealing with conflicting views and approaches
- preventing precipitous action and allowing time and opportunity for those involved to study a problem
- training and developing people by enabling them to acquire new skills, information, expertise, and contacts

There are also situations in which teamwork may not be the most effective way to get results—for example,

- when no one is interested in or cares about a specific issue
- when there is a crisis or emergency and a decision must be made immediately
- when people enjoy and are more productive working by themselves

In sum, teams *are* an effective method for involving people and capitalizing on their collective energy. They are not a panacea, however. Much must be done to manage teams so that they produce the best results for the organization. Careful attention must be given to how they are structured and what issues are chosen.

There are many benefits associated with team participation. The following are some of the most important ones:

- Team members are more likely to accept and carry out decisions, since they know where the decisions came from.

- Many heads are better than one. When teaming is accomplished effectively, there is synergy. The pooled wisdom, knowledge, talents, interests, and information of the team is more valuable than the sum of the individual parts. The task of managing a school organization is very complex; no one person has a wide enough range of skills or knowledge to perform this task successfully.

- Achieving group goals through team synergy can be even more satisfying than realizing individual goals.

- Teaming provides an opportunity for individual members to develop supportive, caring relationships as they work through problems and issues.

Factors That Aid or Impede Teams

There are a number of factors that can aid or impede team performance. Such factors include the following.

Organizational Structure. The structure of the organization within which the team operates—the organization's policies, systems, and program—will have either a positive or a negative impact on team performance. For example, an adequate reward system will enhance teamwork, as will a policy of open communication. Inadequate facilities, services, or materials, on the other hand, will discourage it.

Team Charge. A team must have a purpose; without one there is no need for the team to exist. A general charge, therefore, should be given to team members—both in writing and orally—in order to preclude any misunderstandings. Members should then be able to set their own goals and control how they are to be achieved.

Team Roles. When roles within the team are clearly defined, less conflict will occur, issues will be resolved more easily, and team meetings will operate more smoothly. Some questions related to team roles are

- How much power do team members have to make a decision?

- Are there any issues or situations that team members are not allowed to address?

- How are issues to be resolved when there is a conflict?

Teamwork Processes. Team members must know how to operate as a team and must be trained in ways of working together. If, for example, team members are expected to solve all problems via consensus, the full membership must be trained in the consensus process. Although the team leader has primary responsibility for ensuring that meetings are functional, all team members must contribute to keeping meetings interesting and effective if the team is to succeed.

Team Relationships. The quality of interaction among team members to a large degree determines the degree to which the team will be effective in achieving its charge. Poor relationships will eventually doom a team. The quality of interaction involves morale, harmony, and absence of conflict, all of which depend upon team cohesiveness, which in turn depends upon three variables:

- Similarity of team members in terms of characteristics and traits. Team members who have similar interests and training and share similar attitudes about work are likely to communicate freely and openly, and such communication facilitates team cohesiveness and interaction.

- Frequency of contact. Assuming that team members are prone to interact, the more scheduled and unscheduled meetings there are, the more interaction there will be.

- Behavior predictability. Team cohesiveness is enhanced when team members are able to predict with a fair degree of reliability what other members will do under any given set of conditions. The better team members know one another, the more they are able to predict behavior and attitudes.

Can teams be employed as effectively in public education as they are in the best-run companies? The answer is an emphatic "yes"—but only under certain conditions.

- The superintendent, administrators, and supervisors must be committed to a humane manner of managing the school and the school district.

- Each team must be allowed a great deal of autonomy to plan, control, and perform its job as the

153

team sees best. This means that many of the decisions hitherto made by principals and supervisors must be left to school people from all levels. The principals and supervisors must believe that by sharing power they are making better use of it.

- Team members must be kept constantly informed about how the school and team are progressing. Timely and good feedback is an absolute necessity.

- Each team member must be trained to perform a variety of skills. The team must be perceived as a responsible group dedicated to performing not just one specific job but all of the activities required to achieve a particular goal.

Changing Roles. When a school is organized into teams, the role of the principal changes dramatically. The principal should become trained in the principles and practices of teamwork and team building in order better to perform his or her role as a support staff member, a coach, a counselor, a teacher, a facilitator, and a leader. He or she can successfully build teams by

- allowing teams to operate independently and to discover for themselves the best ways of dealing with situations

- helping teams achieve a small success before tackling large problems

- providing warm words of reassurance and otherwise helping teams to withstand difficult times and the setbacks that inevitably occur from time to time

- helping individual team members who have encountered some kind of difficulty, either job-related or personal

- directly intervening only when absolutely necessary—for example, when a team has lost any sense of direction and needs help getting back on course

- demonstrating caringness, trust, and intimacy through actions, words, and deeds.

The ability of the leader is undoubtedly the most important factor in determining team effectiveness. In order to effect positive team behavior, team leaders need to

- encourage every team member to become involved in the team process

- refrain from dominating and prevent other team members from dominating team discussions

- enable team members to satisfy their personal goals while achieving team goals

- maximize strengths and minimize weaknesses of all team members

- work to obtain synergy

- avoid minimizing the importance of any team member

- remain alert and open to new ideas and suggestions and be willing to learn from individual team members

- recognize and reward team members for their participation

- encourage input by actively soliciting advice

- face up to resistance by bringing it out in the open and identifying why the opposition exists, without placing blame on any one party

- tell the whole truth

- reassure tense or nervous team members by encouraging them to vent and explore their true feelings

- establish high standards and expectations and act as a model to be emulated

Training helps team leaders perform their jobs in the best way possible. Training in such areas as group dynamics, group conflict, problem solving, and so forth is also helpful to team members. Such training could take place during the summer, with or without extra compensation.

Evaluation

The success of teams is heavily dependent upon a continual process of evaluation and feedback. Team members evaluate one another's contributions to the teams in terms of their teaching, human relations skills, participation in training and development, community involvement, and so forth. (Usually if a team member's performance needs improvement, the team members are responsible for helping that member improve. They may decide, for example, that the person should be given a day off to participate in training outside the school district.) In addition, team members evaluate the effectiveness of the team as a whole as well as that of the team leader. The principal also evaluates the team leader, who in turn evaluates the principal. Teams also evaluate the contribution made to their performance by support staff.

In order to further ensure that the team process is working, the central administration team (composed of the superintendent, assistant superintendents, and others) should periodically meet with each team. At this meeting, the team should give a presentation on how the team is progressing. This meeting may or may not be very grueling, depending on the efforts of the team to achieve excellence. The principal, acting as a support person, should clarify issues for the team and assist in identifying problems. At these meetings, decisions should be reached by all parties present concerning the need for additional support services, changes in the team's budget, new solutions to problems, and so forth.

One final thought about teams: The success of teams depends on trust. In fact, Raymond Dreyfus once said that management by teams is the ultimate expression of trust. Having teams make decisions, for example, sometimes requires more time than would be needed if decisions were made by one person; thus there must be trust, which is supported by the evidence, that the decisions made will be of equal and probably better quality. In sum, in order for the team process to work, management personnel must trust that all people at all levels of the organization not only are well qualified but are interested in doing a good job and are capable of managing themselves on an individual and collective basis. An important side effect of this trust is that people's self-respect and self-esteem will be enhanced, and their perception of management improved.

Strategies for Achieving Excellence

- Build teamwork by having teams do the following:

–Prepare a mission statement. Have team members write their own versions of a mission statement. These should be discussed and then the consensus decision-making process used to arrive at the team's mission statement. Because of the interaction that this process encourages, it is an excellent way to begin building effective teamwork.

–Develop a code of conduct. A code of conduct is a list of guidelines governing a team's attitudes and actions. Instead of using the common brainstorming method to produce the code, it may be better for the team to use the nominal group process and to reach a consensus as to the final document.

–Set goals. The mission statement should provide a basis for team members to interact further in order to establish a set of goals. The goal-setting process itself should afford team members an opportunity to learn more about themselves and to understand each other better.

–Review and discuss job responsibilities. Team members should write a paragraph outlining their individual responsibilities and be prepared to discuss the salient features. The ensuing review and discussion should help all team members to understand better their own and one another's job functions.

• To address short-term problems, organize and use temporary teams, being sure to

–choose the people most appropriate for fulfilling the charge of the team

–inform team members why they were chosen for the task at hand

- Develop strong permanent teams by

    –starting with temporary teams and making them permanent only if they are successful

    –giving teams the necessary information, training, and tools to do their job

    –stimulating interest in teamwork through competition

    –insisting that teams not take on too much too soon

    –making certain that teams have short-range (thirty- to sixty-day) as well as long-range objectives to meet

    –requiring a minimum of paperwork and assigning a secretary to help with any clerical work

    –issuing no procedures or policies

    –encouraging all team members to give all that they can no matter what their position in the school district

    –giving praise, encouragement, and credit to the team

    –relating on an intimate and personal basis with team members.

Give Teachers Autonomy and Encourage Intrapreneurship

> Churches, universities, and schools need to be innovative fully as much as any business does. Indeed, they may need it more.
> —PETER C. DRUCKER

Each year our public schools lose students to one of their formidable competitors, the private schools. According to Peter Drucker in his recent book *Innovation and Entrepreneurship*, "the public schools are shrinking in almost every American community. But despite the decline in the number of children of school age as a result of the 'baby bust' of the 1960s, a whole new species of nonprofit but private schools is flourishing." He goes on to say, "The public school in the United States exemplifies both the opportunity and the dangers. Unless it takes the lead in innovation it is unlikely to survive this century, except as a school for the minorities in the slums."

In short, our public schools must innovate or they will fade away. And in order to innovate effectively, they must give school people more freedom, because when people are given more freedom—when they are allowed to manage themselves—they show more initiative in fulfilling both personal and organizational goals. In other words, with more autonomy school people are more likely to show intrapreneurship—the ability or tendency to develop innovative principles, practices, programs, and products *within* an established organization. It appears that the higher the degree of education and maturity of the people involved, the more intrapreneurship they show. If this is indeed true, then individual and team self-management should work wonders in our schools because of the high level of education and maturity of school people.

Unfortunately, many school districts seem to persist in applying Douglas McGregory's Theory X approach, which postulates that the average employee must be directed, controlled, coerced, and even threatened with punishment to make sure he or she puts forth maximum effort. In contrast, many of the best-run companies are advocates of McGregory's Theory Y, which holds that the average employee is capable of assuming responsibility, possesses great potential, and will act responsibly if properly motivated. These companies further believe that giving their people freedom to manage themselves is the key to maintaining a competitive edge. Kollmorgen Corporation embodies this statement of philosophy, which reads in part, "The process of innovation—so important to a high technology company—needs the input of many individuals, since any one individual can comprehend only a small part of the total available knowledge. In a free environment, each individual can contribute his ideas freely, without having them stifled by the ideas of an organizational superior."

Self-Management in the Best-Run Companies

Self-management has been the *modus operandi* at People Express since the company was founded in June 1982. Its people are free to move around and become familiar with every job in the company in order to decide what job they would like to do. There are no rigid job requirements, and

161

training is emphasized. A certain quality of performance is maintained by constantly offering feedback so that people know how well they are meeting their objectives. Douglas Strains, chairman of Electric Scientific Industries, believes that most of the time management merely gets in the way of people, and therefore diminishes performance effectiveness. He believes that a manager is like a lens, helping people to focus their energies in a common direction. To this end, he has developed a "matrix organizational structure," at the top of which is a management team composed of the managers in charge of every division. Problems are discussed by this management team, and decisions are arrived at by consensus.

Donnelly Mirrors operates on the principle that people will be responsible if they are given the opportunity to make decisions for themselves. Donnelly puts this principle into practice by allowing individual and team self-management. The company is divided into teams of ten employees. Each team sets its own objectives within the context of the overall goals of the company, and each team member is expected to perform not only his or her own primary job but also those of other team members. Teams are linked to other teams by team leaders.

Butler Manufacturing Co. has a plant in Story City, Iowa, which is run by several self-managing teams composed of from five to twelve people. These teams decide for themselves how to allocate human resources to meet production objectives, and they are accountable for the results. Teams are also responsible for testing and inspecting both individual parts and the completed products, and for routine maintenance and repairs of tools and equipment. Teams receive production and performance records on a daily basis so that they are aware of the extent to which they are fulfilling specified objectives. Teams not meeting their objectives are encouraged to get assistance from other teams. Formal weekly meetings are held by each team; at these meetings behavioral and disciplinary problems among other things are discussed and resolved. Once a month, unit coordinators and other representatives attend one of the weekly meetings to share information and to review the previous month's performance results. Quarterly meetings provide similar feedback and keep teams up to date concerning conditions. Teams also participate in the assessment and hiring process.

Problems of Self-Management

Individual and team self-management are not without problems. Following are some of those which school districts will no doubt experience.

- Self-management means that more time will be needed to arrive at decisions. However, once decisions have been made, the quality of the decisions tends to be either equal to or higher than that of those made prior to self-management. In addition, the decisions are better implemented because of the psychology of ownership.

- Some people may find it difficult to function in teams because individual performance becomes subordinate to team performance, and they therefore no longer have the opportunity to stand above the crowd.

- Autocratic principals will be reluctant to share power with school people and will find it difficult to adapt to their new role as a leader who coaches and counsels rather than directs. Some school people, too, find it difficult to function within a school environment that provides for increased autonomy and self-management because they are used to having an authority figure.

- In some situations, traditionally minded people may find it difficult to go along with ideas and suggestions initiated by self-managed individuals and teams.

- Like other methods of achieving excellence, self-management will require a great deal of patience, guts, hard work, knowledge, training, and perseverance.

The Value of Self-Management in Education

What will individual and team self-management mean for schools? It will mean essentially four things:

- School people at all operating levels will be permitted to make many decisions hitherto reserved for administrators and supervisors—decisions concerning, for example, the duty schedule, performance reviews, the instructional program, monitoring of student performance, staff and student attendance requirements, and problem solving. My experience has convinced me that in most areas, many heads are usually better than one.

- Feedback will improve. Team members will be kept constantly informed about how the job and team are progressing both through their own self-assessments and through the counseling and coaching of the principal.

- Each team member's talents, strengths, and interests will be utilized to the maximum and his or her weaknesses minimized. This will reduce the likelihood that individual teachers will transfer their own deficiencies on to students, which is a common occurrence today.

- Self-management and greater autonomy will make school people's jobs more challenging and enable them to fulfill higher-level human needs such as the need for self-esteem and self-actualization. As a result, they will perceive their jobs as more uplifting and rewarding.

One of the main reasons for the success of the best-run companies is the self-management that prevails in decision making. It is effective in producing excellence because the managerial state of mind is conducive to making it effective. The excellent managers who run these companies assume that the people at all levels are sufficiently well qualified to do their job in a correct manner. They also assume that the people have the interest of the company at heart, and therefore they don't have to devote time, expense, and energy to hiring supervisors to monitor and review performance continually. They really believe that their people possess the initiative, intelligence, and training to put into effect individual and team self-management.

When superintendents give principals increased autonomy, which leads to individual and team self-management, the superintendents are saying in essence that they believe school people can manage themselves—they will perform their jobs in a satisfactory manner even if they are not closely supervised while they work, and they don't need to have their functions, responsibilities, and duties explained on a step-by-step basis.

How to Infuse Self-Management

An important essential difference between teams in public education and in the best-run companies lies in how they are used. In school districts teams are used either to study a situation or to perform a service. In the best-run companies teams are used to solve problems and to achieve results. In other words, company teams are results oriented, whereas school teams tend to be process oriented.

Given that the administration is committed to providing increased autonomy to school people, how can self-management become a reality in a school district? Below is described a field-tested program to follow when infusing individual and team self-management into a school district, as well as a discussion of problems to avoid. Both the principal and the team should enter into this program without an expectation of overnight success.

The best grade or department should be selected to test the feasibility of implementing self-management. A school champion should be selected as team leader. An executive or program champion who will report directly to the superintendent should be designated to work with the initial team and principal to plan and launch the initial self-management program and to make it work. The superintendent should clarify the program and address any questions, reservations, or doubts in the minds of those participating and not participating in the initial program. The team should spend some time discussing the strengths, talents and interests of individual members in order to determine how to make the best use of them. Weaknesses and dislikes should also be explored to determine where additional training and development may be necessary.

The team should be given intensive training. Areas of training should include methods of problem solving (such as that used by quality circles), conflict resolution, consensus decision making, group dynamics, peer review, and planning, as well as any areas recommended by individual team members. This training program should cover two to three weeks.

Consideration should be given to retaining a consultant. If a consultant is retained, he or she should be a hard-nosed practitioner with extensive experience in specific areas, not merely a theorist.

A meeting should be conducted at which the principal and team members come to some agreement as to the number of students to be assigned to the team, the team's objectives and performance standards, conduct of the performance evaluation program, a school duty plan, student and teacher attendance, and so forth.

There should be a meeting some time in August to develop a one-week plan for implementing self-management. At this meeting an attempt should be made to anticipate any problems that are likely to arise, and to consider possible solutions. The implementation plan should provide for daily free time so that the team as a group can meet to decide on the day's activities for individual team members and students.

Now the plan should be implemented. Any problems that arise must be solved, and progress reviewed regularly. A consultant should be used on an as-needed basis. During the course of the school year, the team should meet frequently with the building principal and less often with the superintendent and other school administrators to inform them of the progress of the project.

An outside consulting firm that has had some experience with evaluating teams should be asked to assess the project. Based on the firm's evaluation, a decision should be made as to whether or not individual and team self-management should be implemented in all schools.

If the decision is affirmative, a tersely written implementation plan should be prepared, and a meeting called to familiarize everyone with it. The intent of this meeting should be to explain how each person fits into the plan so as to diminish as much as possible any insecurity. The superintendent should begin the meeting. There should be no doubt as to the superintendent's commitment to this program as a first step to achieving excellence.

The general introduction to self-management should include the following points:

- Self-management will not weaken the union's position but will enable all parties to co-exist more harmoniously.

- Standards of performance will be high; self-management is implemented to maximize the potential of individual team members.

- Under self-management the principal will function more as a teacher and guidance counselor than as a boss, and egalitarianism will be practiced throughout the school district.

- Self-managed teams will be responsible for the total education of their students, and therefore will be expected to design schoolwork policies and procedures and determine individual and team assignments. Teams will also be responsible for taking care of discipline problems.

- Training and development are ongoing processes critical to the success of self-management.

- Communication and continuous feedback through survey questionnaires, team meetings, school meetings, districtwide meetings, and interaction with central administrators are key components of self-management.

- Self-management has to be worked at—it can only become a reality with proper training and experience over a period of time.

- Self-management is not only a process and a program but a way of life—a philosophy of school management that will help the school district to achieve excellence.

The Self-Management Structure

Under a team organizational structure, all jobs in a school fall into two categories: teaching and support teams. The principal and the central administration are in the support team category. Each self-managed teaching team should consist of the teachers within a given grade or subject, and should include no more than eleven members. (A group of twelve teachers, for example, should be divided into two teams of six.) I recommend that elementary school teams be organized according to grades and secondary school teams according to subject. Team leaders should be either appointed by the principal or selected by the team membership. Each team is then put in charge of a group of students. Each teaching team should be responsible for the following critical areas:

- planning and implementing the instructional process so as to improve students' learning and growth

- monitoring attendance of both team members and students

- preparing the schedules of team members and students

- formulating short-range objectives and performance standards to help realize the school district's long-range goals

- developing a program to review, monitor, and improve individual and team performance

- deciding upon and arranging for various training and development activities

- providing whatever activities are necessary to guide students properly in school and toward a vocation

- determining when and how support staff should be used

- preparing and justifying the team's budget, as well as approving all expenditures (for substitutes, training and development, and so forth)

- solving individual, team, and buildingwide problems

The support teams are responsible for anything and everything necessary to help teaching teams to fulfill their purpose. All teams are expected to be creative and innovative in all their activities and decisions, to work collectively and in coordination with other teams, to utilize the skills and talents of all their individual team members, and to strive to provide the best instructional program possible.

Implementing Self-Management

Each teaching team decides on the educational program of each student in the block of students assigned to it. At times, a support team consisting of guidance personnel will work with the teaching team to plan the educational schedule of students. At other times, a support team consisting of psychologists may work with the teaching team to improve teaching effectiveness. Support teams should not be retained in the school if they cannot demonstrate their value to teaching teams.

Teaching teams will find self-management rewarding and fulfilling only if the environment is supportive. The following conditions must be met in order for the environment to be conducive to self-management:

- School work must be meaningful—not just in the eyes of school administrators, but in the eyes of the teaching teams.

- Teaching teams must be given genuine responsibility for performance results.

- Teaching teams must receive immediate feedback concerning their daily progress toward goals and objectives.

Underlying these conditions are five others:

- Teaching teams must be trained to perform a variety of functions hitherto reserved for school administrators.

- Teaching teams must have sufficient autonomy to carry out the total job. For example, they must teach, as well as plan and control the job of teaching.

- Teaching teams must share power with school administrators and must reap the benefits associated with sharing power.

- Teaching teams must provide information on a daily basis as to how well or how poorly the team is performing.

- Teaching teams must be willing to design, process, and appropriate tools, to receive training on the functions to be done, to set standards, to upgrade resources, and to do anything else necessary to achieve excellence.

I believe that giving teachers autonomy is a viable alternative to the voucher system, which is again gaining popularity as one method for achieving excellence in America's schools. If competition is the name of the game, my suggestion would be to produce competition not only among school districts, but also among teams of teachers and among schools within the school district. Such three-way competition can greatly enhance the school district's ability to achieve and maintain excellence.

Intrapreneurship

When teachers are given autonomy, they are expected to engage in individual and team self-management—that is, to plan, control, and perform, either on an individual or a team basis, the instructional process for educating students. The highest form of self-management is intrapreneurship—developing innovative products, programs, and services *within* an established organization. Autonomy and intrapreneurship are inseparable, and both are necessary to achieve excellence in education.

Intrapreneurship will work in education only if policies, rules, regulations and practices of the school district are not allowed to limit the activities of intrapreneurial units. At times the superintendent may have to go to the commissioner of education to get approval for a particular intrapreneurial project. Thus all school people including the commissioner must understand the value of intrapreneurial ventures in education and how they can be meaningful in assisting a school district to achieve excellence.

If teachers are to become intrapreneurs, they must be given the freedom to act on their own. Gifford Pinchot III, author of *Intrapreneuring*, identifies a number of "freedom factors." These freedom factors were derived from considering what the people who actually did the work needed to get the job done. The underlying principle is that organizational management should be based on observing problems from the bottom up and not from the top down. I maintain that the presence or absence of these freedom factors will determine to a large degree how successful a school district is in achieving excellence, because these freedom factors are the foundation for enabling school people to satisfy their higher-level needs. Only when we are able to produce a school environment that meets these needs will we be able to achieve excellence. Below is a list of freedom factors that pertain specifically to education, some of which I added because I felt that they were appropriate.

- Self-selection. Much of the work performed in teams should be based on the functions that individual team members elect to perform. It is assumed that teachers will select those roles and functions with which they feel comfortable because of their individual interests, talents, and skills. Other members of the team must respect the selections made and do whatever is necessary to accommodate them.

- Autonomy. Team members must be permitted to perform their jobs in their own way and must not be hampered by having to explain their actions and to request permission.

- Tolerance of risk, failure, mistakes. Innovations cannot be achieved in a work environment where people are fearful of making mistakes and are reluctant to assume risks. All support individuals and teams must be expected to tolerate risk, failure, and mistakes. Traditionally, school administrators required well-studied and well-planned attempts to develop an innovative idea. Today, creative solutions are so vitally needed that school administrators must encourage multiple tries with less careful preparation.

- Discretionary resources. Teaching teams need discretionary resources to explore and develop new ideas. Discretionary funds may be needed for experimentation with new instructional approaches. At times, it may be necessary for the superintendent to give the entire team time off to finalize the development of an innovative product, or to temporarily assign support staff to accommodate the needs of the team. All teams must be free to make use of the school district's resources, even if these resources are not located within the building in which the team is located. If a vendor with which the school district has had a long-lasting relationship cannot supply a much-needed resource, the team should have the option of looking elsewhere.

- Cross-functional responsibilities. Teams should have full responsibility for planning and developing innovative products, programs, and services.

- Freedom from turfness. New ideas usually cross the boundaries of existing patterns of the school organization. Therefore, some people may attempt to block an innovative idea because of envy. Such counterproductive behavior must not be tolerated.

- Freedom to duplicate effort. Two teams in the same school district should not be prevented from exploring the same idea. However, it would be a sound practice periodically to bring the two teams together so that each can learn from the other.

- Absence of limits. Regardless of who may be affected by the solution, all teams should be encouraged to explore ideas that may help improve the instructional process.

All intrapreneurial teams need a sponsor; that is to say, they need some person or group to be the protector of the idea the team is exploring. Although the school principal should be one of the sponsors of any team operating in his or her school, other sponsors will also be required. Basically, sponsors are needed on two levels: within the school building to see to the day-to-day support needs of the teams and within the central administrative office to fend off major attacks that might threaten the innovation.

A sponsor is different from a mentor. A mentor is concerned with training and education. A sponsor is concerned with technical problems, promotion options, ways to help present an idea, and behind-the-scenes maneuvers needed to protect an innovation.

A person selected to become the sponsor of an idea should be ready, willing and able to do three things: help acquire the necessary resources, help get money from the budget allocation for innovative projects, and help detect and fend off political attacks.

The ideal project sponsor is

- a highly respected person in the central administrative office

- a central administrator or supervisor who was once a member of a team that produced a successful innovation

- a highly respected community member

- a godfather or executive school champion

- a highly regarded professor of education

What are the characteristics of ideal intrapreneurial teaching teams?

- They don't have preconceived ideas about what work is beneath them.

- They are thinkers and doers, planners, controllers, and performers.

- They are extremely dedicated team members.

- They are guided by the needs of their students and feel personally responsible for seeking solutions to problems.

- They are self-determined goal seekers who often do things that no one asks them to do.

- They have high standards for themselves and their students.

- They tend to be confident about the level of team members' skills and about their ability to overcome mistakes and failure.

176

- They are inclined to assume risks to complete a project.

- They set not only short-range objectives but long-range goals, knowing full well that it is what is accomplished in the long haul that is important for achieving excellence.

How do teaching teams select ideas for creating innovative projects to improve the instructional process? Programs and products come from students' needs and teams' needs. Students' needs may become apparent as a result of day-to-day teaching, interviewing students, or soliciting ideas from others. At times, teachering teams will work on an idea that someone within the team suggested in an attempt to facilitate the instructional progress. At other times, an idea may surface as a result of another idea. Regardless of where it comes from, the idea should accommodate the skills and experience of team members and should inspire team members to become more than what they ever hoped to be.

Stew Leonard has a way of generating ideas from his people who work at Stew Leonard's Dairy Store. He takes about a dozen of the people with him to visit a store of one of his competitors. While at the store, his people are requested to look for a new idea that could be implemented immediately upon arriving back at the job. The individuals who come up with the first idea are admitted to the One Idea Club. While in transit from the competitor, the group is not permitted to say anything negative about the competitor. All of their attention is to focus on generating ideas that can be useful for the company. Ideas that are accepted are reported in the company's newsletter.

School districts can use this technique when a team of teachers is sent to a district to observe innovative practices. I personally used this technique when I first became superintendent. Teachers and administrators in my district did a considerable amount of traveling around the nation; our traveling budget must have been every bit of $125,000. Individual teachers and administrators were responsible for studying specific details. For example, one person was designated to observe techniques used to individualize and personalize instruction, another person was responsible for observing the instructional media center, another person was in charge of conferring with students, and yet another was responsible for getting teacher reaction. At the end of the day and sometimes during lunch, the group would discuss its observations and make recommendations as to ideas and programs that could be emulated in our school district. I found that the best part of the visitation was the discussion during which notes were compared and ideas were shared.

Consequences of a Failure to Foster Intrapreneurship

The experiences of the New Jersey Department of Education and the New York City Board of Education provide two examples of the consequences of a failure to foster intrapreneurship.

The Educational Improvement Centers. In 1982, Saul Cooperman became Commissioner of the State Department of Education in New Jersey. One of his first moves was to ask AT&T and Rutgers University to assist him in the reorganization of the Department of Education. Although at the time it seemed to be a good idea to contact AT&T—after all AT&T was one of the largest corporations in America—with the benefit of hindsight, I see that AT&T was not the most appropriate organization to emulate. AT&T had virtually no competition; therefore it did little in terms of adopting the new management techniques and programs (such as egalitarianism, intrapreneurship, consensus management, management by walking around, and so forth) that characterize many of the best-run companies. Whereas companies such as Hewlett-Packard, Procter & Gamble, 3M, and IBM are required to seek new products, new programs, new practices, new methods, and new principles to gain an edge over their competitors, AT&T's management approaches were basically the same as they had always been. (I certainly don't blame the commissioner, however. I was on his advisory team at the time and didn't realize the limitations of AT&T.)

The representative of AT&T encouraged the advisory team to establish distribution centers instead of the autonomous units that had existed under the previous administration. The distribution centers became known as regional curriculum services centers. The main office of the Department of Education served essentially as the brain of the Department, providing innovative products and services, while the regional curriculum services centers delivered these products and services. Before the commissioner's reorganization, products and services were both developed and delivered by units known as educational improvement centers. These centers were governed by a board of directors composed of a cross-section of representatives of the area, whose main purpose was to accommodate the needs of its stakeholders. Periodic meetings were held with the parent organization, the State Department of Education, in an effort to coordinate a statewide thrust to improve the educational process of the state. These centers were free to apply for grants to produce creative and innovative products and services that met the long-range goals of the Department and to apply whatever pressure necessary within the Department to meet the needs of their respective geographical locations. Although these centers were partially subsidized by federal, state, and private grants, the State Department of Education provided most of their operating funds. Over the course of seven years, these centers were responsible for bringing into the state of New Jersey nearly $20 million of educational programs and services; for training nearly a million teachers, administrators, board members, and parents; for producing countless numbers of products that were used by both teachers and students; and for remaining abreast of current trends and developments in education and industry and informing their constituents about them. In 1983, as a result of the reorganization, all but one of these intrapreneurial centers were dissolved and replaced with regional curriculum services centers. The one remaining educational improvement center was abandoned by the State Department of Education, made to change its name, and left virtually on its own to assist its constituents to achieve excellence.

It would be well worth the time and effort of all school people to visit the Educational Information and Resource Center, located in Sewell, N.J. to observe the kinds of high-quality programs and services being offered there. Nothing comparable is emerging from any of the new regional curriculum services centers. Even if the commissioner made the shift necessary to change the distribution centers back to intrapreneurial components of the department, it would probably take five to ten years for them to duplicate the level of programs and services that the educational improvement centers once produced in the state of New Jersey.

Harlem Prep School. Located on Eighth Avenue in New York City, Harlem Prep School had an unusual student population—dropouts ranging in age from sixteen to forty-nine. This school developed its own innovative and creative instructional techniques and methods in order to provide a viable education for its students. The success of Harlem Prep School was incontrovertible proof of the failure of traditional education for certain students and the need for such innovative types of educational programs.

The academic program at Harlem Prep encompassed the four subject areas of social studies, African culture, mathematics, and English. Classes were conducted informally in small and medium sized groups, with students grouped around a table or encircling the instructor in movable chairs. Students were continually afforded opportunities to participate in their own learning and the learning of other students. For instance, in English classes, students wrote essays which were then read before the class so that all class members could participate in correcting, modifying, and evaluating the papers. A great deal of material of interest to the students was incorporated into the curriculum through the use of contemporary paperback books relevant to students' life-realities. These books served to encourage the growth of good reading habits. Most classes were composed of no more that fifteen students. Each instructor discussed and presented his or her materials with an air of intimacy and informality. Those students needing further clarification of a point casually directed their comments to instructors, who replied on a one-to-one basis and yet at the same time made clear that other students were welcome to become involved. At Harlem Prep all students were allowed to progress at their own pace. The emphasis placed on the dignity and human worth of each individual contributed immensely to the high motivation which was evident among its students.

All identification with traditional forms of public education was cast out in this unique school, where hungry students were allowed to eat in class, sleepy students were not embarrassed or penalized for dozing in class, and students did not need to ask permission to retire to a rest room to attend to personal needs. The students' response to being treated as human beings was to act as human beings; they did not abuse the humane conditions under which they were permitted to learn.

The school was housed in what had formerly been a large supermarket, located in the middle of a large urban ghetto. Most of its students were black youth from socially, economically, or psychologically disadvantaged backgrounds. Many of these students had been "forced out" of the public school system, but all were still trying to acquire the education necessary to cope with the society in which they lived. So, they came to Harlem Prep where classes were small and imbued with relevance. At Harlem Prep they found sensitive and well-trained teachers who were extremely flexible and created many-faceted approaches to arouse and maintain student interest. There was a free flow of communication between teachers and students in different subject areas so that students were presented with an interdisciplinary approach to learning. In addition, each teacher was expected to serve not only as an instructor, but also as a friend, guidance counselor, and advisor. Harlem Prep was staffed by a cadre of Marymount Sisters and professionals with degrees ranging from masters to doctorate. The school had a long waiting list of outstanding teachers who were interested in having the opportunity to participate in the learning process at this unique school.

If college entrance is the determinant of success of a school, Harlem Prep ranked among the top. In 1967-68, all of its thirty-six graduating students were accepted into institutions for higher learning in the United States, including the University of California at Berkeley, SUNY Buffalo, Fordham University, Vassar College, Wesleyan University, Long Island University, SUNY Stony Brook, and Harvard University. Twenty of these students were surveyed after the first semester of studies, and the majority were found to have maintained grade averages of A or B, with the lowest mark being a C+.

What made Harlem work? Perhaps the best reason was given by the school's director, Mr. Carpenter: "Every kid in this school gets warmth, affection, and love—and they give it too."

One would think that a highly successful educational project such as Harlem Prep School would be allowed to thrive. Not so. When the authorities of the New York City Board of Education took control of the school, they saw fit to incorporate the board's culture into the culture of the Harlem Prep through administrative policies, rules, edicts, and limitations. Harlem Prep had worked because it produced an educational culture that accommodated the needs and interests of students who found it impossible to cope in a traditional educational culture. Without the benefit of a unique educational culture the program met its demise. Had Harlem Prep been left to function as an intrapreneurial unit within the New York City school system, it would probably still be successfully meeting the needs of students. We must learn not to tamper with success.

Strategies for Achieving Excellence

- Develop an Intrapreneurship Honor Roll, which lists the school district's intrapreneurs along with the innovative ideas they contributed.

- Include a provision in the school district's statement of philosophy that expresses the district's commitment to giving people autonomy and encouraging intrapreneurship.

- Establish an innovative budget from which grants can be made to school teams that have good ideas for achieving excellence. Develop guidelines to be used as a basis for giving the grants.

- Train teachers to use the nominal group process rather than brainstorming as a way to generate ideas. Reason: Research has demonstrated that the nominal group process yields not only more ideas but also more varied ideas and ideas of better quality.

- Boost team morale (and thereby the team's sense of intrapreneurship) by conducting pride sessions in which the team members are given the opportunity to congratulate themselves for things the team has done well. The session should end with a discussion of things the team could do even better.

- Organize a Student Action Team (SAT) consisting of four or five adults involved with the school district—for example, a teacher, a guidance counselor, an administrator, and a parent—as well as four or five students. Give them the mission of identifying and solving critical problems in the middle or secondary school.

- Ask your state's department of education to approve the establishment in your district of an intrapreneurial center, which would develop programs and services in the following areas:

  –alternative education for difficult students
  –preparation for the Scholastic Aptitude Test
  –training and development for school people
  –preparation and publication of innovative educational materials.

NOTES

Lesson 1: Support School Champions

Most of the substance of this lesson came from two sources: Terrence E. Deal and Allan A. Kennedy, *Corporate Cultures: The Rites and Rituals of Corporate Life* (Reading, Mass.: Addison-Wesley Publishing Co., 1982), pp. 37-57; Thomas J. Peters and Robert H. Waterman, *In Search of Excellence: Lessons from America's Best-Run Companies* (New York: Harper and Row, 1982), pp. 202-234.

I also interviewed a number of educators around the nation trying to identify efforts made by school districts to support school champions. My endeavors produced disappointing results. All of the twenty-two school administrators that I interviewed indicated either that they did not have support systems or that they did not know how to identify them.

Lesson 2: Adopt a Suggestion Program

I gathered much of the material for this lesson from Robert Levering, Milton Moskowitz, and Michael Katz, *The 100 Best Companies to Work for in America* (Reading, Mass.: Addison-Wesley Publishing Co., 1984). I also had a lengthy conversation with an official of the National Association of Suggestion Systems to corroborate my statements, and to inquire as to how many school districts were adopting suggestion programs.

1. IBM's 1983 and 1984 Annual Reports provided helpful information on its suggestion programs. In addition, any references within this lesson to a school or

district are from intensive interviews with school administrators in charge of suggestion programs.

2. An interesting article on a suggestion program in Japan is included in Kenichi Ohmae, *The Mind of the Strategist—The Art of Japanese Business* (New York: McGraw-Hill Book Co., 1982), pp. 58-59.

Lesson 3: Move from Philosophy to Culture

One of the best books on organizational culture, a book I referred to quite frequently when writing this lesson, is Terrence E. Deal and Allan A. Kennedy, *Corporate Cultures: The Rites and Rituals of Corporate Life* (Reading, Mass.: Addison-Wesley Publishing Co., 1982), pp. 3-36. Another book that I found helpful was Craig R. Hickman and Michael A. Silva, *Creating Excellence—Managing Corporate Culture, Strategy and Change in the New Age* (New York: New American Library, 1984). I also found the following helpful: Matthew King and Jon Saphire, "Good Seeds Grow in Strong Culture," *Educational Leadership,* Vol. 42 No. 6 (March, 1985), pp. 67-74.

Lesson 4: Intensify and Personalize Communications

The substance of this lesson was based in part on Thomas J. Peters and Robert Waterman's book, *In Search of Excellence—Lessons from America's Best-Run Companies* (New York: Harper and Row, 1982). In addition I also relied on Thomas J. Peters and Mary Austin's most recent book, *A Passion for Excellence—The Leadership Difference* (New York: Random House, 1985). I also used as references various documents of the best-run companies which they very graciously shared with me. At times I spoke to various top-level managers to clarify a point or to receive additional information. Whenever I referred within a lesson to the achievements of a specific administrator or other school person, the information I report is from an interview with one or more central administrators in that school district.

Several articles that I found extremely useful when researching this article were Lawrence A. Bennigson, "Managing Corporate Culture," *Management Review* (February, 1985), pp. 31-32; Edwin L. Baker, "Managing Organizational Culture," *Management Review* (July 1980), pp. 8-13; Howard Schwartz and Stanley M. Davis, "Matching Corporate Culture and Business Strategy," *Organizational Dynamics* (Summer, 1981), pp. 30-48; Von Saphier and Matthew King, "Good Seeds Grow in Strong Cultures," *Educational Leadership* (March 1985), pp. 67-74.

Lesson 5: Reach Decisions by Consensus

For general information about consensus, perhaps the best book is by Michael Avery, Brian Auvine Barbara Streibel, and Lennie Weiss, *Building United Judgment: A Handbook for Consensus Decision Making* (Madison, Wis.: The Center for Conflict Resolution, 1981).

1. William Ouchi, *Theory Z—How American Business Can Meet the Japanese Challenge* (Reading, Mass.: Addison Wesley Publishing Co., 1981), p. 44.

2. For an excellent discussion of participative methods of decision making and their use in industry, see Edgar H. Schein, *Process Construction* (Reading, Mass.: Addison-Wesley Publishing Co., 1969).

3. Much of the information in this lesson concerning how some of the best-run companies use consensus

came from Robert Levering, Milton Moskowitz, and Michael Katz, *The 100 Best Companies to Work for in America* (Reading, Mass.: Addison-Wesley Publishing Co., 1984).

Lesson 6: Become Close to Kids

Much of the substance of this lesson was obtained from the numerous documents that eighty-seven of the best-run companies shared with me.

> The strategic curriculum is a new idea which I think deserves a great deal of study and action. In order to stay abreast of future needs of students, school districts must critically review current trends and developments, and analyze their curricula in terms of these trends and developments to determine where gaps exist, and then make efforts to close the gaps. If school districts do this, they will be able better to prepare their students to cope with the future.

Lesson 7: Give New Emphasis to Training

The substance of much of this lesson was obtained from documents of many of the best-run companies.

The substance of much of this lesson was obtained from documents of the best-run companies. Two books I found useful were: Harry Levinson, *The Excellent Executive—A Psychological Conception* (New York: New American Library, 1968) p. 176 and James O'Toole, *Vanguard Management—Redesigning the Corporate Future* (New York: Doubleday & Company, 1985) p. 291.

Lesson 8: Make Sure Superintendents Are Generalists

I found highly informative the well-written book by Harry Levinson and Stuart Rosenthal, *CEO—Corporate Leadership in Action* (New York: Basic Books, 1984). It gave me some insights into how some of the most noted chief executive officers in the United States developed plans to grow their own top managers. I also referred to Robert Levering, Milton Moskowitz, and Michael Katz, *The 100 Best Companies to Work for in America* (Reading, Mass.: Addison-Wesley Publishing Co., 1984), pp. 108-111.

Lesson 9: Hints for Achieving Excellence

The substance of this lesson was arrived at through my experiences and readings. I owe a great deal to the American Management Association's publication, "Management Review."

Lesson 10: Recognize and Reward Excellence

Some of the practices for recognizing and rewarding excellence described in this lesson were obtained from two sources: Thomas J. Peters and Robert H. Waterman, *In Search of Excellence: Lessons from America's Best-Run Companies* (New York: Harper and Row, 1982) Robert Levering, Milton Moskowitz, and Michael Katz, *The 100 Best Companies to Work for in America* (Reading, Mass.: Addison-Wesley Publishing Co., 1984).

Lesson 11: Achieve Excellence Through Teams

Much of the information in this lesson about what the best-run companies are doing with teams was extracted from Robert Levering, Milton Moskowitz, and Michael Katz, *The 100 Best Companies to Work for in America* (Reading, Mass.: Addison-Wesley Publishing Co., 1984). I also found useful a book by Raymond Dreyfack, *Making It in Management: The Japanese Way* (Rockville Centre, N.Y.: Farnsworth Publishing Co., 1982); James Short, *Working in Teams: Practical Manual for Improving Work Groups* (New York: AMACOM, 1981).

In addition, some of the material in this lesson came from my book, James Lewis, Jr., *Excellent Organizations— How to Manage Them Using Theory Z* (New York: J. L. Wilkerson Publishing Co., 1985). I also interviewed a number of people from four of the best-run companies to confirm my information as to how their companies are using teams.

Lesson 12: Give Teachers Autonomy and Encourage Intrapreneurship

Much of the substance of this chapter was obtained from Robert Levering, Milton Moskowitz, and Michael Katz, *The 100 Best Companies to Work for in America* (Reading, Mass.: Addison-Wesley Publishing Co., 1984). I also made good use of materials sent to me by many of the 100 best-run companies.

One of the most interesting and informative discussions concerning self-management is in Raymond Dreyfack, *Making It in Management: The Japanese Way* (Rockville Centre, N. Y.: Farnsworth Publishing Co., 1982), pp. 87-90, 154-164.

1. Peter Drucker, *Innovation and Entrepreneurship: Practices and Principles* (New York: Harper and Row, 1985), pp. 10, 186.

2. Gifford Pinchot, III. *Intrapreneuring—Why You Don't Have to Leave the Corporation to Become an Entrepreneur* (New York: Harper and Row, 1985), pp. 195-199.

3. The essence of my discussion came from Gifford Pinchot III: *Intrapreneuring—Why You Don't Have to Leave the Corporation to Become an Entrepreneur* (New York: Harper and Row, 1985), pp. 143-159.

• GLOSSARY •

Autonomy. The power to decide for oneself how one is going to manage an entire process.

Career Path Program. A long-range plan for successive on-the-job learning experiences involving a variety of functions, geared to improving an employee's skills and value to the organization.

Certified Quality Circle Facilitator. A person who has completed a minimum of five days or forty hours of comprehensive training by a certified facilitator in the various phases of the quality circle concept and has passed an extensive examination.

Circle Leader. An employee, usually a unit supervisor, who is trained in the quality circle concept, and who provides leadership to circle members as they work to solve problems.

Circle Members. Employees trained in the quality circle concept who work together to solve job-related problems.

Consensus. A decision-making process whereby members of a team (group) cooperatively arrive at a mutually acceptable decision which all participants agree to support.

Culture. An integrated pattern of human behavior that is exhibited by an identifiable group of people and includes thought, speech, action, and artifacts.

Entrepreneurship. Developing innovative principles, practices, and products *outside* the confines of any established organization.

General School Administrator. A school administrator, usually on the central administration level, who has had at least one year of actual experience in the areas of personnel, business administration, curriculum, and instructional administration.

Inculcating a Philosophy. The process of impressing upon people certain macroprinciples that should govern their behavior and attitudes.

Intrapreneurship. Developing innovative principles, practices, programs, and products *within* an established organization.

Job Rotation. A formal plan for assigning employees to different jobs so they can get training in a variety of functions.

Mission. The general purpose of an organization.

Nominal Group Process. A method of organizing a group's interactions that allows group members maximum involvement in the making of decisions.

Performance Evaluation. A critical assessment of work performed, conducted formally or informally by an individual or group.

Quality Circle. A group of three to eleven persons who meet voluntarily, usually for one hour a week, to identify, analyze, and devise solutions to job-related problems in the group's area of responsibility; verify the solutions; recommend them to superiors; and implement them when possible.

Shared Values Statement. A statement identifying the values that are or should be held by all members of an organization.

Statement of Philosophy. A document that spells out the socio-economic purposes, mission, beliefs, and goals of an organization.

Training. An organized activity designed to improve an employee's job performance and therefore his or her value to the organization.

Training Strand. A continuum of training activities designed to prepare an employee to perform one or more specific functions.

• BIBLIOGRAPHY •

Ash, Mary Kay. *Mary Kay on People Management*. New York: Warner Books, 1984.

Auvine, Brian, Betsy Densmore, Mary Extron, Scott Paole, and Michael Shanklin. *A Manual for Group Facilitators*. Madison, Wis.: The Center for Conflict Resolution, 1978.

Avery, Michael, Brian Auvine, Barbara Streibel, and Lennie Weiss. *Building United Judgment: A Handbook for Consensus Decision Making*. Madison, Wis.: The Center for Conflict Resolution, 1981.

Bartov, Glenn. *Decisions by Consensus*. Chicago: Progressive Publisher, 1978.

Bennett, Dudley. *TA and the Manager*. New York: AMACOM, 1976.

Blakeslee, Thomas R. *The Right Brain: A New Understanding of the Unconscious Mind and Its Creative Power*. Garden City, N.Y.: Anchor Press/Doubleday, 1980.

Blanchard, Kenneth, Patricia Zigarmi, and Drea Zigarmi. *Leadership and the One-Minute Manager*. New York: William Morrow and Co., 1985.

Blanchard, Kenneth, and Spencer Johnson. *The One-Minute Manager*. New York: William Morrow and Co., 1982.

Christopher, William F. *Management for the 1980's*. New York: AMACOM, 1980.

Cribbin, James J. *Leadership —Strategies for Organizational Effectiveness*. New York: AMACOM, 1981.

Cribbin, James J. *Leadership —Your Competitive Edge*. New York: AMACOM, 1981.

Cummings, Paul W. *Open Management: Guides to Successful Practice*. New York: AMACOM, 1980.

Deal, Terrence E., and Allan A. Kennedy. *Corporate Cultures: The Rites and Rituals of Corporate Life*. Reading, Mass.: Addison-Wesley Publishing Co., 1982.

Delbecq, Andre L., Andrew Van de Ven, and David H. Gustafson. *Group Techniques for Program Planning: A Guide to Nominal Group and Group and Delphi Processes*. Glenview, Ill.: Scott Foresman and Co., 1975.

Dreyfack, Raymond. *Making It in Management: The Japanese Way*. Rockville Centre, N.Y.: Farnsworth Publishing Co., Inc., 1982.

Drucker, Peter F. *Innovation and Entrepreneurship—Practice and Principles*. New York: Harper and Row, 1985.

Feinberg, Mortimer, Robert Tanofsky, and John J. Tarrant. *The New Psychology for Managing People*. Englewood Cliffs, N.J.: Prentice-Hall, 1978.

Gardner, James E. *Training the New Supervisor*. New York: AMACOM, 1980.

Geneen, Harold D. *Managing*. New York: Doubleday and Company, 1984.

Gilder, George. *The Spirit of Enterprise*. New York: Simon and Schuster, 1984.

Goldberg, Philip. *The Intuitive Edge: Understanding and Developing Intuition*. Los Angeles: J. P. Tarcher, Inc., 1983.

Hickman, Craig R., and Michael A. Silva. *Creating Excellence—Managing Corporate Culture, Strategy, and Change in the New Age*. New York: New American Library, 1984.

Hughes, Charles L. *Goal Setting: Key to Individual and Organizational Effectiveness.* New York: American Management Association, 1965.

Iacocca, Lee. *Iacocca—An Autobiography.* New York: Bantam Books, 1984.

Ingle, Sud. *Quality Circles Master Guide.* Englewood Cliffs, N.J.: Prentice-Hall, 1982.

Iwata, Ryushi. *Japanese Style Management: Its Foundation and Prospects.* Tokyo: Asian Productivity Organization, 1982.

Kanter, Rosabeth Moss. *The Change Masters—Innovation and Entrepreneurship in the American Corporation.* New York: Simon and Schuster, 1983.

Kelsey, Morton T. *Caring—How Can We Love One Another?* New York: Pauleat Press, 1981.

Keyes, Ken, Jr. *Handbook to Higher Consciousness.* Marina del Rey, Cal.: De Vorss & Company, 1975.

Knowles, Malcolm and Hulda. *Introduction to Group Dynamics.* Chicago: Association Press, 1972.

Kotter, John P. *The General Managers.* New York: The Free Press, 1982.

Krathwohl, David R., Benjamin S. Bloom, and Bertram B. Masia. *Taxonomy of Educational Objectives. The Classification of Educational Goals. Handbook II: Affective Domain.* New York: David McKay Co., 1956.

Leavitt, Harold J. *Managerial Psychology.* Chicago: The University of Chicago Press, 1964.

LeBoeuf, Michael, *The Greatest Management Principle in the World.* New York: G. P. Putnam's Sons, 1985.

Lee, Sang M. *Management by Multiple Objectives: A Modern Management Approach*. New York: Petrocelli Books, 1981.

Levering, Robert, Milton Moskowitz, and Michael Katz. *The 100 Best Companies to Work for in America*. Reading, Mass.: Addison-Wesley Publishing Co., 1984.

Levinson, Harry, and Stuart Rosenthal. *CEO—Corporate Leadership in Action*. New York: Basic Books, 1984.

McCormack, Mark H. *What They Don't Teach You at Harvard Business School*. New York: Bantam Books, 1984.

Miller, Lawrence M. *American Spirit—Visions of a New Corporate Culture*. New York: William Morrow and Co., 1984.

Mink, Oscar, James M. Schultz, and Barbara P. Mink. *Developing and Managing Open Organizations*. Austin, Tex.: Learning Concepts, 1979.

Myers, M. Scott. *Every Employee a Manager*. New York: McGraw-Hill, 1981.

Nadler, Leonard. *Developing Human Resources*. Austin, Tex.: Learning Concepts, 1970.

Ohmae, Kenichi. *The Mind of the Strategist*. New York: McGraw-Hill, 1982.

Ouchi, William. *Theory Z: How American Business Can Meet the Japanese Challenge*. Reading, Mass.: Addison-Wesley Publishing Co., 1981.

Pascale, Richard T., and Anthony G. Athos. *The Art of Japanese Management: Applications for American Executives*. New York: Simon and Schuster, 1981.

Peters, Thomas J., and Nancy Austin. *A Passion for Excellence—The Leadership Difference.* New York: Random House, 1985.

Peters, Thomas J., and Robert H. Waterman. *In Search of Excellence: Lessons from America's Best Run Companies.* New York: Harper and Row, 1982.

Pinchot, Gifford, III. *Intrapreneuring—Why You Don't Have to Leave the Corporation to Become an Entrepreneur.* New York: Harper and Row, 1985.

QC Circle Headquarters. *QC Circle Koryo—General Principles of the QC Circle.* San Jose, Cal.: QC Circle Headquarters, 1980.

Quick, Thomas L. *Person to Person Management.* New York: St. Martin's Press, 1977.

Randolph, Robert M. *Planagement—Moving Concept into Reality.* New York: AMACOM, 1974.

Schonberger, Richard J. *Japanese Manufacturers' Techniques: Nine Hidden Lessons in Simplicity.* New York: The Free Press, 1982.

Short, James H. *Working in Teams: Practical Manual for Improving Work Groups.* New York: AMACOM, 1981.

Steiner, George A. *Strategies Planning: What Every Manager Must Know.* New York: The Free Press, 1979.

Toffler, Alvin, *The Adaptive Corporation.* New York: McGraw-Hill, 1985.

Toole, James, *Vanguard Management—Redesigning the Corporate Future.* Garden City, N.Y.: Doubleday and Company, 1985.

Tregoe, Benjamin B., and John B. Zimmerman. *Top Management Strategy.* New York: Simon and Schuster, 1980.

• INDEX •